Tommy Cooper

Tommy Cooper
Just Like That

Jeremy Novick

CHAMELEON

First published in Great Britain in 1998 by
Chameleon Books
an imprint of André Deutsch Ltd
76 Dean Street
London W1V 5HA

André Deutsch Ltd is a VCI plc company

www.vci.co.uk

Design: Will Harvey for JMP Ltd
Picture research: Karen Tucker for JMP Ltd

The right of Jeremy Novick to be identified as the author
of this work has been asserted by him in accordance with
the Copyright, Designs and Patents act 1988

10 9 8 7 6 5 4 3 2 1

Origination by Digicol Link (London)

Printed in Italy

A catalogue record for this book is available from the
British Library

ISBN 0 233 99411 4

For Isaac Levi

And so to the thanks.

Thanks to Nigel Billen. It's one of those few times that you say 'without whom it wouldn't have been possible' and it's true. Thanks also to Rob for being Rob, Mal for being so surprised when I told him that it was late and to John for not bothering. Thanks to John Gill – my fate's in your hands, John. Thanks to Dennis Kirkland for being so sweet, Roy Addison, Eric Sykes (who cared), and Norman Wisdom for taking the time. And thanks to Darryl Butcher and Laurie Bellew, Margaret Forwood and Patrick Stoddart for being supportive.

Thanks especially to Gilly, Elly, Maxwell C Wolf and Lexa for being there. More than a boy ever hoped for.

And thanks to Grandpa Louis for maintaining an interest.

Finally, to Paul Tomlin. You've no idea, but you made this possible. A diamond.

The Prologue

WHEN I SAT DOWN TO WRITE THIS BOOK, I tried to think about Tommy Cooper and what it was that he did. I tried to look at it as dispassionately and objectively as possible: you know, be professional. So I read loads of books, but that was useless. So I decided to watch some tapes of him doing what he did. Tapes of him on stage, tapes of him on television.

The first gag I saw him do was this:

Tommy Cooper: 'Doctor, you've got to help me. It hurts when I go like that [lifts arm up].'

Doctor: 'Well, don't do that.'

While the studio audience were laughing like drains, and I was still trying to work it out, Cooper rummaged around a table-top strewn with what looked like jumble-sale tat and found a joke pair of glasses which had a pair of plastic antlers attached to them. He put them on.

'Horn-rimmed glasses.'

Now, am I wrong or is that rubbish? Tell me, am I wrong?

I'd say to people, 'I'm writing a book about Tommy Cooper,' and, nine times out of ten, after they'd done the obligatory 'uh-huh-huh-huh' Cooperesque laugh, they'd say, 'How are you going to do that?'

What do you mean, how am I going to do that? Well, I've taken a bit of time off work and I'm going to try to talk to…

'No. How are you going to write a book about Tommy Cooper?'

Huh?

'Just like that!'

It was funny when they did that, but not as funny as the bloke I interviewed who did the whole interview in 'Cooper'. You try having a proper discussion with an ordinary-looking bloke who's sitting there talking into a microphone doing the whole 'uh-huh-huh-huh' routine. And you try going home after that and transcribing the interview tape.

So, still I tried to work out what it was that he did. The more that I thought about it, the more it seemed to me that the only answer was, 'not very much'. He had his act, which was pure music hall, or more accurately, pure variety. The fez, the magic tricks that went wrong, the embarrassed hamming it up to the audience: it was all a great turn, but really, that's all it was: a turn. Yes, it was a superbly thought-out turn. Yes, it was a superbly executed turn. Yes, the timing was exquisite, the nuance perfect. But it was just a turn.

The more I thought about it, the more I became convinced I was missing something. This was a man unanimously and universally described as 'a legend'. This was a man to whom all the comic greats you could think of bowed. This was a man who inspired both his public and his peers. Even allowing for the fact that he's dead, even allowing for the fact that his generation of comedians never – ever – say anything but good things about each other, what intrigued me was the way that his peers spoke about him. Eric Sykes, for example, was absolutely in awe of Cooper. They were great mates, yes, but he had an instinctive respect for the man. And Sykes, it was stressed to me time and again while writing this, bowed to no one when it came to comedy.

There was a warmth, but it was a warmth that was tempered with a reverence, a genuine respect. OK, allow for the fact that they're all essentially theatre people, the Tarbucks, the Monkhouses, the Milligans, and therefore susceptible to a touch of luvvie-ness, but there was none of that. There's none of the old (out come the hankies) 'he died on the stage; he died for us' nonsense. It was all a lot more earthy than that, a lot more real. The way that they spoke about Tom was special. (It was always Tom: like they were speaking about a mate. Or a brother.)

It's often the case that when you're writing a book, the subject matter gets under your skin. I remember writing a football book – well, it was only loosely about football: it was about Spurs – and after a while I noticed that obviously I was inserting the word 'obviously' into every sentence. It was the same here. I resisted the 'Just like that', but I found myself almost subconsciously walking around going 'uh-huh-huh-huh' and shrugging up my shoulders. It was like a cross between Mike Yarwood's impression of Ted Heath and the worst Tommy Cooper you've ever seen. 'Uh-huh-huh-huh.'

Tommy Cooper. It was a curious thing, but he got under my skin. ◼

'I haven't said anything yet'

'He did a great after-dinner speech at the Water Rats, This great big man just stood up. That's all he did. He just stood up and the place was in absolute hysterics at a man standing up. Now, I don't care how much you study comedy, you can't define that, that ability to fill a room with laughter because you are emanating humour. After several minutes of solid laughter, he turned round to his wife and said "I haven't said anything yet," and the whole place went up again.'

— Paul Daniels

DENNIS KIRKLAND WAS TOMMY'S long-time producer at Thames TV – he worked with him for 20 years, starting off as floor manager and ending up as producer/director. Kirkland, a stalwart of ITV comedy, overseeing such names as Eric Sykes, Benny Hill, Jim Davidson and Freddie Starr, told me a Cooper story. It was a classic Cooper story, part of Tarbuck's repertoire, too. 'I remember being in Blackpool one summer and Morecambe and Wise were doing a summer season and Jimmy Tarbuck was there and, I think, Harry Worth. They were all doing summer seasons and Tommy Cooper came to do a week in one of the clubs. One night, everyone decided to go and watch him, not to tell him that they were coming or anything, but just to sit quietly at the back and watch and maybe heckle a bit. Anyway, within minutes of Cooper coming on stage, a waiter carrying a tray of full beer glasses walked past us and tipped the whole thing over. The noise… It was pandemonium. Tommy just stood there on the stage and didn't say a word. All the lads around me were coming up with smart one-liners, trying to guess what Tommy would say because, of course, this sort of thing was manna from heaven for a comedian. Well, he just stood there and for minutes he didn't say a word.

After a while he looked up and said "Uh-huh. that's nice." Of course, the place just fell apart.'

I wasn't there, but I feel the same as that audience. Just saying the name, just saying those two words, evokes an involuntary smile, a smile that's as warm and as open as is possible when you're dealing with someone that you don't know, someone you've never met, someone who's a 'TV star'. Tommy Cooper.

You should never look at a light bulb and ask yourself, 'How does that work?' Look, if the Lord wanted us to know, he'd have given us an instruction book. As it is, it's enough that it works. Be happy with the light.

It's like that with comedy. Who knows why it's funny? Who can say? The only thing that you can be sure of is that if you try to work out why it's funny, you'll let the humour – the joy of the involuntary smile – slip through your fingers like a bag of water.

You can line people up to try to analyse it…

'I knew Tommy for thirty years and he was one of the great funny men. He was absolutely fantastic. No other comic would work with him, he was too good. He had this fantastic expression. I don't know what the impressionists are going to do now. Tommy was a giant of comedy, a British WC Fields and he will be irreplaceable. I've never met anybody who disliked him as a man. If you didn't like Tommy Cooper the comic, you didn't like comedy.'

Eric Morecambe

…but the more you look…

'What tickled me about Tommy Cooper was that he was so irreverent about the human condition. Everything about the human condition is so laughable and that's where he touched the funny bone in me… The seriousness of actors has always left me cold, but people like Eric Morecambe, Tommy Cooper and Ken Dodd have always got to me because they laugh at themselves, they laugh at us. I think what he did was make us laugh at the fool in ourselves.'

Sir Anthony Hopkins

…the more you find people saying that Cooper's funny…

'Cooper was the greatest instinctive, natural clown I've ever seen or met. I remember being taken as a kid by my parents to the summer season at the Bournemouth Winter Gardens where Tommy was topping the bill. It was a vast, aircraft hangar of a place. Tommy strolled very nonchalantly across to far stage-right where he did three minutes of stand-up and got his laughs. Then, as we all knew he was going to do, he walked right over to the other side of the stage. It seemed to take him about five minutes. Then he did the same three minutes of stand-up, and the jokes seemed even funnier. Only Tommy could do that sort of thing.'

John Fisher, writer/producer of the Heroes Of Comedy series.

Which, really, is what you already knew. Maybe we should know to leave it to Eric Sykes, a man henceforth to be known as 'The Guvnor'.

'He said to me, "You people say that all I have to do is to go out on stage and people will laugh. But if they only knew how much it took me to go out on that stage." I said to him, "For God's sake, Tom, don't what ever you do analyse it. Just thank God that He gave you that gift.'"

Eric Sykes

'**REMEMBER HIS ACT?**' said Dennis Kirkland. 'He didn't used to come on for 10 minutes. What happened was, at the club or wherever it was he was playing, they'd announce, "Ladies and gentlemen, the great Tommy Cooper!" and the music would start up – he'd always come on to the Sheikh Of Araby – and then nothing. The audience would start to giggle a little bit because they know its Tommy. So where's Tommy? Probably still in the dressing room having a pint. Then they'd do it all again. The announcement, the song. It used to go on forever and in the end it would just fade and the audience would be wondering what was going on. Suddenly this voice would say from backstage, "Uh-huh. I suppose I'd better go on stage," and the house would go up. They'd collapse. He'd do this whole dialogue in the dark about trying to get out of the dressing room – "They must have locked the door. No, it's a broom cupboard" – he's talking rubbish, the audience is crying and the man hasn't even gone on the stage. Now that is talent. All there is is a spotlight on a dark stage, waiting. And he would start telling his gags – 'I went to see my doctor the other day. I had to. He wasn't well' – and the audience would be roaring and he wasn't even on stage. Then he'd walk on backwards and turn round with

mock surprise, "Oh, there you are." I mean, that's courage.'

Courage? Yes. Courage and inspired genius coupled with a raging self-confidence that tells you you'd get away with it. It's also mad. Surreal. A lot of the stuff that Cooper used to do was like that. It was what Monty Python would have been like if they'd been educated at the Glasgow Moss Empire rather than Cambridge.

'He used to have a white gate on stage and he used to walk on tiptoe through the gate for no reason at all,' continued Kirkland. 'In the end, he used to have people crying with laughter, and he'd just opened the gate. But you see that's an obscure thing to do, it's way out – you know? I saw him once,' continued Kirkland, 'and he had two tables on stage and the audience was crying and he hadn't done anything. And he decided that they weren't level and so he moved one a little bit and then they still weren't level, so he moved the other one and this went on forever and people were falling over at this idiot. It doesn't even sound funny, but when he did it it was funny.

'It's truly surreal, but a lot of comics wouldn't do it. Mind you, a lot of comics have made a good career of doing Tommy Cooper doing gags like that. Mike Yarwood used to say, "If I'm ever not doing well I just throw in a bit of Cooper."'

It's funny, isn't it? More 'sophisticated' comics shying away from doing the school-playground humour that Cooper indulged in but hijacking him – and those gags – when they were desperate.

Ironies abound. Here's another one. Like some dinosaur rock band, Tommy Cooper was kicked away by the new,

young comedians of the late 1970s and early 1980s, young bucks dragged into view by the punk-inspired revolution. These were alternative comedians – an alternative, you presume, to the dinner-suited Coopers of this world whose idea of a stage set was a theatrical curtain. Like that curtain, they were a relic of the music halls. Time for bed, granddad…

The irony was that the new breed – and this is no disrespect to them, it's just the way it is – were puppy careerists whose idea of alternative was BBC2.

Beneath the dinner-suited exterior and the ITV prime-time slot, Cooper was a thousand times more subversive. He might not have spent time telling gags about farts and period pains like some of those young bucks, but he was genuinely surreal. Cooper didn't have to get involved in all that rude stuff. Listen, this was a man whose hero was Max

Miller. One of the foundation stones of his stage act was Ophelia, a 'song and dance' number that Miller first performed in 1937. He had a picture of Miller hanging up in his lounge. The chances are that he'd heard more gags about farts and period pains than anyone. As Miller might have said, when these young ones came along, Cooper had a choice: Should he go back the way he'd come or should he toss himself off?

TOMMY COOPER. What was he? A comic who looked like a magician or a magician who looked like a comic? The latter probably. Because whatever it was he looked like, it was nothing like a magician.

'One of the reasons that people found him so amazing, was because you'd never seen a magician, a conjurer, who wasn't little and dapper and neat, who didn't have small clever hands and cunning little hands pretending to be drunk or sophisticated, pretending to be something that enabled them to put over their magic. Suddenly there was this man incapable of doing any magic with hands like big bunches of bananas and great clomping steps and you thought that this man can't possible do any tricks and when it turned out that he was getting them all wrong the joke was that you were watching him at all.'

Bob Monkhouse

The visual thing was, obviously, hugely important. As Clive James said, 'Well, he did have a flying start with the way he looked.' What did he look like? Six foot four cubic, size 13 feet, the immaculate dinner jacket and attendant bits, the ridiculous fez with the tassels hanging down the front, the funny tufty bits of hair sticking out of the sides: it was a ridiculous get up. Neck down, perfectly respectable. Neck up…

There are so many descriptions of Cooper's extraordinary physical appearance – and the face that once made Spike Milligan comment, 'The face was a call for help, wasn't it?' – that to add to them seems churlish. My two favourites are *The Times* obituary writer's description of Cooper as 'the crag-featured comedian whose profile seemed carved from a combination of a relief map of Norway, the north face of the Eiger and an Easter Island sculpture.'

The other is Clive James's: 'A mutant begot by a heavyweight boxer in a car crash in Baghdad.' It's funny that James should mention the bit about a boxer because Tommy Cooper actually was. He was a good heavyweight and an army champion in the Horse Guards, so good that he was offered a contract to turn professional. His size, his sheer bulk… it's not something you're going to argue with. Imagine it: you're a heavyweight boxer on the make and your manager fixes you up with a bout against Tommy Cooper. Actually, it's difficult to picture this image of the huge Tommy Cooper in full boxing regalia without that image turning around and hamming it up. 'Uh-huh-huh-uh.'

Naturally, he had an 'I used to be a boxer' routine. This is how it went:

'I used to fight in the same style as that other Cooper.'

Henry?

'No, Gladys. I used to frighten the life out of my opponents by using an old trick – I bled all over them. I spent so much time on the canvas that my nickname was Rembrandt. I made a fortune by selling the advertising on the soles of my boots.'

Were you ever stopped?

'Only once. It was for speeding.'

Boom boom.

AGAIN WITH THE appearance, things weren't all they seemed. You looked and what did you see? This great, big, hulking clod-hopping giant with a huge body and feet that really were like plates of meat. But that wasn't really the story. Like Eric Morecambe, Ernie Wise and countless other comics who had learnt their trade stomping the boards, Cooper was astonishingly graceful. 'The feet, the head, it's all wrong, but you know he was so light on his feet,' said Dennis

Kirkland. 'He was very graceful, he used to do a little pirouette, a little turn, almost like a ballet turn or a Muhammad Ali shuffle and go across to the next bit of nonsense.'

In a sense, Tommy Cooper was nothing more and nothing less than a comic magician. It was his awareness of the limitations of his own magic that produced his most brilliant comedy. You knew that his tricks wouldn't work, that his sleight-of-hand would be as sleight as a brickie's hod and that the flowers would only pop out of the vase when he finally managed to free the spring mechanism. The disappearing clock-in-the-box disappeared only to fall out of the back of the box. The multiplying bottles routine is interrupted only by Tommy leaning under the table to get more bottles. Every gag is an anarchic kick at the conventions of showbiz professionalism. (Yet his biggest fans were his fellow professionals. It's not surprising, really. He had the bravery to do what they'd have loved to.)

He deliberately parodied the magic and his verbal humour displayed the same lack of reverence. The jokes would fall out of his mouth with little regard for conventional comic notions like timing and flow, although, of course, it was the same as with the magic: to break the rules you've got to know the rules. Cooper had as much idea of – and respect for – comic timing as any conventional stand-up and it was only because his timing was so impeccable that he could get away with it.

Of course, it wasn't all timing and form and theoretical know-how and the fact that he looked ridiculous. As much

as anything, Cooper drew on an enormous reserve of chutzpah. To walk on stage, look at the audience and say, 'Watch, watch,' and then pull a watch from your pocket – that takes chutzpah.

It's very different to, say, Paul Daniels, who isn't a comic magician like Cooper but is a magician who uses a bit of comedy. Where Cooper demonstrates that he loves the game and then proceeds to take the whole thing apart, Daniels uses his humour simply to distract the viewer. It's a prop used to support. Give Cooper a prop and the first thing he'd do would be kick it away.

It's a bizarre idea. A man shows an unwavering ability to get his trade wrong; worse, he shows us all how he gets his trade wrong – and then he expects to be rewarded by his public. It's a genuinely subversive idea. And, like the best subversives, he looked completely straight. Well, conventional. Well, you know what I mean.

Daniels, incidentally, idolised Cooper. After Tommy died, there was a showbiz charity do, an auction of some of Cooper's bits and pieces and Daniels was the auctioneer. When it came to his cape, Daniels went through the whole routine, right up to the going, going, gone – except that right at the end, he said 'Going, going, gone – to Paul Daniels.' He paid £500 over and above the highest bid and said afterwards that it wouldn't have mattered who bid or how much they had bid, he was going to have that cloak. ◼

Part human, Part insane

'In destroying the magic, he elevated it ... (If) he'd have kept doing just the magic, the world would have missed a great clown but Tommy, by poking fun at it – though never nastily – made audiences aware that magic could be enjoyed.'

– Paul Daniels

COOPER'S DELIBERATE SABOTAGE

didn't limit itself to his performance. It infected all around him – he made sure of that.

In his book *TV Mythologies*, Albert Hunt pointed out that Cooper's attitude – his chaotic rehearsals, his penchant for refusing scripts, repeatedly changing the running order, missing those crucial little chalk marks, inserting new routines and throwing around one-liners – ensured that the recordings were unfocused, that shots weren't framed in, how shall we say, an orthodox manner. It's all part of that same idea of debunking.

It's debatable whether television ever truly captured the madcap comic genius of Tommy Cooper. I know that sounds like one of those 'nostalgia ain't what it used to be' clichés that everyone peddles in books about characters from the past but in the case of acts that grew out of the music halls, it's often true.

It's like Morecambe and Wise. They were hugely successful out there in theatreland and pounded the boards for over half a century, drawing the crowds in and sending them home exhausted and happy. They were also the most popular British light entertainment performers there have ever been, legendary figures who attracted huge ratings and persuaded the biggest stars of stage and screen to appear on their shows. But the Morecambe and Wise who got in their Transit van and schlepped up and down the M1 were very different to the Morecambe and Wise who bounced out of the magic box in the corner of the front room. They had to be. What was right for the stage wasn't necessarily right for the telly.

For someone like Tommy Cooper, it was the same story. Too often, producers would try to put him in sketches and situations that just weren't right. OK, Kirkland once allowed Cooper five minutes to do that 'non-appearing' routine that he used to start his stage shows with but it didn't really work on television. Five minutes of a black stage lit only with a single spotlight.

'Tom wasn't at his best on TV. You had to see Tom on the stage because then he was really good. He could grab an audience like no one. He was like Frankie Howerd in a way,

their métier was the stage. They were too big for TV.'

Eric Sykes.

Even if you don't include his shows from the latter part of his life, from the late 1970s and early 1980s, when the effects of life were taking their toll, it could be argued that TV didn't capture Cooper at his best. In a sense, though, how could it? Cooper was a stage performer, an artist who'd been formed in front of a live crowd, an artist who dealt in energy and who fed off the energy that a crowd gave him.

'He once gave me a piece of advice. he said to me, "Never work in front of a mirror," and you can see that in the way that he went about his business. He realised that if you practise in front of a mirror you are performing essentially to yourself, and you can see that in some acts; they are their own biggest fans. Tom used to practice in front of a blank wall, imagining that there was an audience there, and that comes through in his act – he's always giving out to the audience. There was nothing self-regarding about the way he went about his business.'

Bob Monkhouse

In a sense, it was a wonder that Cooper was as successful on television as he was. He was notoriously late for rehearsals, and even when his internal clock did work and he did appear – or, more likely, when his wife Gwen's nagging and hectoring worked – he played his cards very close to his chest. Well, he would, wouldn't he? He's a magician.

He never used to tell directors exactly what was going on. He'd never explain to fellow performers – the straight men, the stooges   exactly how things were going to pan out. Often when you saw him on the telly, walking around the stage picking up this from the table, looking at it, putting it down, picking up something else, when he was going through that whole routine, he was really considering what trick to do next, what gag to throw away.

That isn't to say though that he was under-prepared. He was meticulous in his preparation. Like another of his heroes, Stan Laurel, Tommy was, when it came to the thing closest to his heart, a very serious bunny.

He was an absolute perfectionist and practised his magic until he got it perfect, but he didn't rehearse in any conventional sense and couldn't be tied down to the conventions of either the TV studio or the theatrical stage.

It's curious but it's a similar story to John McEnroe. He was the most naturally-gifted tennis player of his generation. He played with an instinctive grasp of the game: when you watched him play you could see that he didn't go through that process that other tennis players go through. The ball comes at them and, in their head, they run through the options, what shots they could return it with. McEnroe didn't have that thought process. He just played the shot. Reading about McEnroe, it seems that he loved playing tennis. He could be out there playing for hours and hours, but weight training? Stamina training? Fitness training?

Both Cooper and McEnroe had an innate gift which they loved doing – what did they need to worry about anything else for. ?

If McEnroe found himself in a tricky situation, he'd improvise. A running backhand lob volley such as the one against Connors in 1984, for example. No one else would have thought of that, and even if they did, no one would have dared do it, and even if they did, no one else could have pulled it off.

If Cooper found himself in grief, he'd rummage around on his table, pick up a joke saw-through-the-head, put it on and say, 'I've got a sore head. Uh-huh-huh-huh.' Again, no one else would have thought of that, and even if they did, no one would have dared do it. Even if they did, no one else could have pulled it off.

'HE LOVED IT,' said Dennis Kirkland. 'Absolutely loved it. You see, Tommy didn't have to perform. It wasn't that he had to do something. The funny thing was, he'd walk through the door and you'd be roaring with laughter and he hadn't done anything.' Here comes that old emanating humour thing again.

'If I came in and said, "I'd like a cup of tea," I'd get a cup of tea,' said Kirkland. 'If Tommy did it, everyone would just fall about. He'd walk in, have a look around, start moving everything on the table around, shuffle around a bit and – you see, you're laughing now and I haven't said anything.

'He was funny because you loved him. That's why he's the best and everyone says he's the best. He's the most naturally funny man we've ever had. He was just naturally funny. He couldn't go wrong, even though sometimes I watch tapes of the shows and some of the sketches are rubbish. They're far too long and unstructured, but you'd be riveted because Tommy was in it — other people wouldn't get away with it.

'His jokes. "I had to see my doctor the other day. I had to. He wasn't well." I mean, what a dreadful line that is, but what can you do? "I said, 'I keep thinking I'm a dog.' He said, 'How long have you thought that?' I said, 'Ever since I was a pup.' He said, 'Get on the couch.' I said, 'I'm not allowed.'" It's nonsense, you know, but it has audiences on the floor.'

It was rubbish. Somehow it was reassuring to hear someone else say that, someone who was so close to Tom, someone who thought he was a genius. Where is the line between rubbish and brilliant?

'I don't know. His rubbish was brilliant. Only he could get away with it.'

Maybe his rubbish was brilliant because he got away with it?

'You think of what he did and you wonder how he got away with it. He was so childish. He was a child. He was a great big baby.'

Of course he was a child. 'Richard Briers said that he was just like a child who had caught a bubble on his hand and his fascination with it was unbelievable, and he's absolutely right,' said Kirkland. 'Tommy is like a kid because he giggled at what he did.'

'His joy was to amaze and delight like a child would,' said Bob Monkhouse. 'There was a side of him that I don't think ever grew up. What grown man would walk around with a tea bag in his pocket just so that he could stuff it in a taxi driver's top pocket if he should happen to take a cab? It was enough for Tom to know that he'd discover it later,

he didn't have to be there to see it. It was a joke that you'd buy from a joke shop and that was the type of joke that Tommy loved.'

Ah, the famous tea bag gag. Tommy would get out of a cab and, after paying, stuff something in the cabbie's top pocket and thank him. 'Have a drink on me.' The cabbie would drive off with thoughts of the big star stuffing notes into his pocket. When he got home and looked he'd find a tea bag. Again, it's mad as pie but very, very funny.

But he had a wicked sense of humour, too. Roy Addison told me about one of the routines he used to do.

'He used to choose someone from the audience — he'd be very careful to choose the right person — and he'd ask them to hand him a note, a £5 or £10 note. Then he'd ask them to look at it and tell him how many songs they could make from what they saw. And so they'd go through them, and there'd be, oh, Rule Britannia, maybe a few others. When they said that they couldn't think of any more, Tommy said, "There's one more." And they'd ask what and Tommy would say, "Bits and pieces," and he'd proceed to tear the bank notes into tiny pieces. He'd be very careful to choose people who looked as if they could afford it, and it would be hilarious because what could they say?'

Didn't anyone get angry?

'With a story like that to take away?'

I wonder what Thomas Mann would have said about the tea bag gag. Mann once said that clowns are 'basically alien beings… side-splitting, world-renouncing monks of unreason, cavorting hybrids, part human, part insane.' Well, I don't know about that.

You can get carried away, you know, and I'm not sure that Tommy Cooper saw himself as a world-renouncing monk of unreason. A hugely funny comic, maybe, but a world-renouncing monk of unreason? Probably not. 'Uh-huh.'

Tommy Cooper. By all accounts he was one of those rare beasts who was chosen for a life of comedy. As Eric Sykes said, 'I've always maintained that people don't decide to become comics. It's the audience who decide whether they'll become comics. In many cases – like Frankie Howerd, who wanted to be a straight actor but they decreed that he would be a comic, Jimmy Edwards wanted to be a bishop but he was a comic, the same with Tom – they wanted to be something different, but they were so good at what they did that the audience decided that that was the path they'd choose.'

The stories about Tom just tumble out as soon as you mention his name. There's the story about the time Tommy and Miff Ferrie, his manager, had done some gigs in Australia and on the way back they had a stop-over in Tokyo for about four or five hours. Neither of them had been to Japan before so they decided to take a taxi into town and have a quick drive around. The driver could not speak any English and you can just imagine how much Japanese Tommy and Miff spoke. Anyway, the taxi driver ended up driving into a wall because he was laughing so much.

Sir Anthony Hopkins has made a minor career out of being A Fan Of Tommy Cooper and even went as far as to reveal, on The Des O'Connor Show, that he'd based aspects of his character from *Silence Of The Lambs*, Hannibal Lecter, on Cooper.

'Couldn't you see the influence of Cooper in the character?'

Yes, of course. But how did you get that thing with the teeth?

'Just like that.'

Rehearsed? Get out of here. But it doesn't matter. It's a nice tale.

ON 12 MAY 1996, Norman Wisdom unveiled a memorial to Tommy Cooper at Teddington Studios in south-west London, on the same day as Sir Harry Secombe unveiled a bronze statue of Tony Hancock – cutely situated outside Birmingham's regional blood transfusion centre. Along with Joyce Grenfell, Peter Cook, Eric Morecambe and Les Dawson, Tommy has been commemorated by having his own Royal Mail stamp. Not everyone has been so impressed, mind.

In Exeter, they didn't see fit to honour him. 'Snooty civic society bosses' turned down a bid to put a blue plaque on Cooper's childhood home. Chair Hazel Harvey said, 'Tommy Cooper just came and went. We go for more cultural people - like the man who wrote Onward Christian Soldiers.' Yes, Hazel. And, er, what was his name again?

And the stories came with a real warmth. Tom arriving with his two trademark brown paper bags. Tom sitting down, surrounding himself with about eight or so different drinks – water, tea, whisky, juice etc – and taking sips from here and there. Tom sitting down, talking to you and doing a card trick while you were chatting. Everyone I spoke to stressed what a good magician he was, mentioned how he was in the inner Magic Circle. It was his great love. 'He made a joke of his conjuring but his ambition in life was to be the best illusionist in the world,' said Eric Sykes.

What came across was that he had a precious resource and everyone recognised it. It was a quality that made his peers revere him. He inspired an astonished reverence. He had the ability to do naturally what they spent hours rehearsing. And, it seems, he was an incredibly nice bloke. After I'd finished interviewing Eric Sykes, he turned round and said, 'I'm only doing this because of Tommy. I do think that he was the greatest and I think that more recognition is needed, you know. It's very difficult. What I would like you to do when you write this up is tone down what I've said about myself and bring Tommy out a bit more. No, really, because I can assure you I love the man so much and I'm so glad you're writing a book and I really want him to come out, not me.'

How many showbiz types are going to say something like that? I really want him to come out, not me.

But I think that one of the nicest, most complimentary things that I heard about Tom was this. In her book *For The Love Of Tommy*, his assistant (or possibly more – see The Cooper Curse, later), Mary Kay reveals that Thames Television used the recorded audience from Cooper's show as canned laughter for their other shows. 'It was the most natural,' they said.

A man stands on a stage in front of a full-length theatrical curtain. The stage is completely bare. He's wearing a full dinner suit – freshly-laundered white shirt, black bow-tie, crisp white pocket handkerchief. Immaculate. Only his head gives the game away. A red fez sits on his head, the black tassels hanging forward. Little tufts of hair stick out of the sides.

He produces a large red cloth and places it over one of his hands.

'Ladies and gentlemen. Four live ducks.'

He peeks under the red cloth, smiles as though he's a bit embarrassed, fiddles under the cloth a bit and repeats:

'Ladies and gentlemen. Four live ducks.'

He whips the red cloth away to reveal... a large hole in the middle of the table.

'They must have flown off.'

A Red Letter Day

'Well, it might have all gone wrong but at least I got a laugh. Perhaps I should concentrate on that.'
— Tommy Cooper, 1938

TOMMY COOPER WAS BORN on 9 March 1922 in Caerphilly, South Wales. Though technically Welsh, it was Devon that gave him his identity and his faint West Country burr. His father was from Caerphilly and his mother from Devonshire and a few weeks after he was born the family upped sticks and moved to Exeter. There's a rumour that Tommy's father, a poultry farmer, wanted his child to be born in Wales so that, if the child turned out to be a man, he would be eligible to play rugby for Wales. Well, Mr Cooper. Right sex, right size, wrong inclination. The idea of seeing Tommy Cooper in a scrummage… Maybe it's just as well it never happened.

'My father said the day I was born was a red-letter day. He received final demands for the gas, the electricity, rates and half a dozen assorted HP items.'

It's one of life's glorious ironies that the way Tommy arrived in this world was pure Cooper. Nothing went the way it was supposed to go, lines were fluffed and the bits didn't fit. But at the end of the performance what you had was bigger and better than could have been expected. Tommy's mother was seven months pregnant, through the worst bit and rolling along in full bloom. When Tommy's father suggested they go out to the pictures, she thought nothing of it. But on their return… Without going into the details – really, they're unnecessary here and I'm sure you can guess – that night Tommy was born.

Now, you've got to remember that this was 1922 and it might have been this century but it was a different world. The doctor who delivered Tommy didn't hold out much hope for the tiny baby. 'The doctor threw him down on the bottom of the bed and gave him up,' Gwen said later. 'He was such a poor little thing. But his Grandma kept him alive on drops of brandy and condensed milk.'

And he grew up to be Tommy Cooper, six foot four … in each direction. You've got to wonder. He grew up to be Tommy Cooper on a blend of brandy and condensed milk. Imagine how big he'd have been if he'd have been fed the barrage of vitamins and nutrients that babies get today. There is another way of looking at it. Maybe grandma was right. Maybe the old ways are the best. Maybe we should all feed our babies brandy and condensed milk. Maybe all those refined pills and sophisticated potions are actually not so good for us. And then we'd have a world full of… Tommy Coopers. 'Uh-huh-huh-huh.' No. It's not worth thinking about.

The family moved to Southampton but Tommy returned to Exeter to go to college and did what young men tend to do: he hung around. A spell on board a boat as an apprentice shipwright was cut short after he got the sack. And why did he get the sack? Because, obviously, he was caught playing tricks with a magic set his aunt Lucy had given him when he was eight. Why else would you be thrown off a boat? Incidentally, Tommy never did forget his aunt Lucy. On the opening night of ITV, a night that he was an integral part of, he paid tribute to her with the words: 'Hello, auntie. There's just one thing I'd like you to know – I still can't do the tricks!'

It was on that boat, though, that our hero gave his first public performance. At the ripe old age of 16, Cooper stood up in front of a lunchtime audience of riveters, platers and boiler-makers – real men – and set out to distract them from the serious business of eating. Up he got, just like that, and proceeded to dazzle them by producing a series of fancy coloured handkerchiefs from a cylinder and, hey!, what's that behind my ear? Why, it's the ace of spades!

Only, the hankies got stuck in the cylinder and while he was trying to free them what was that that fell out of his sleeve? Why, it's the ace of spades! The audience fell about and the young 16-year-old ran off the 'stage', tears streaming down his face. 'I was in tears at the time. I was so nervous I got stage fright. That's why it all went wrong, because of the nervousness.' It's an obvious irony but the act that caused him to run off crying would in years to come have audiences around the world howling with laughter. If the 16-year-old only knew.

When the tears dried and the embarrassment faded, Tom sat down in his quarters and started to practise again. As he did, a thought crossed his mind. 'I thought to myself,' he later recalled, 'Well, it might have all gone wrong but at least I got a laugh. Perhaps I should concentrate on that.' ▰

'I was with my wife and she was reading a magazine and she showed me a photograph of a fur coat and said "I'd like that." So I cut it out and gave it to her.'

Meet the Gang, 'cos the Boys are Here, the Boys to Entertain You

'Throughout our marriage, my wife has always stood by my side. She had to. We've only got one chair.'

THE COURSE OF TRUE LOVE never did run smooth and all thoughts of showbiz and superstardom — or, at least, the stage and the gruelling Moss Empire circuit — were put on the back burner by the little matter of the Second World War. It's difficult to think of the young Tommy Cooper without conjuring up (sorry) a mental picture of a young lad with Cooper's head, fez and all, sitting on top of it. So when you read a simple sentence like, 'In 1940 he was called to the army and joined the Horse Guards for seven years,' well, you just know that things aren't going to go exactly as the assorted generals would have liked. The phrase 'officers' mess' comes to mind rather too quickly.

What happened? Well, firstly, bear this in mind. Horse Guards are called Troopers and Tommy Cooper the Horse Guard was — honest — Trooper Cooper. Really. They should have stopped there.

There were a hundred guards in Cooper's unit and the scene was like something out of a *Carry On* film. Rows and rows of neatly turned out soldiers standing proudly and correctly next to their horses – and Trooper Cooper, standing there in his army cap with little tufts of hair sticking out, size 13 army boots (which aren't delicate at the best of times) and over-shadowing this horse, which is, well, what? A Shetland pony? A *Steptoe and Son* dray horse?

Day one, it went wrong. Day one. 'I put my foot in the stirrup but the saddle slipped and I ended up underneath the horse's belly. Everyone was sitting on their horse – except me. At first, I couldn't understand it, but it seems that horses don't like their straps on too tight. So they breathe out while you're putting the saddle on and then breathe in just as you're getting on. What you should do is…' Forget it, Tom. It was never going to be a relationship made in heaven.

Cooper's team was sent to the Middle East, to a camp near Suez, and he found himself as near a real war as anyone would want to get. He served with an armoured car reconnaissance unit until he was wounded in the right arm. Typical Cooper, really. Serving in an armoured car unit and getting shot. He did what any self-respecting comic would do: meet the gang, 'cos the boys are here, the boys to entertain you. He joined the concert party and took up entertaining the troops. What choice? Before he could join, though, he had to have an audition. You can almost write this next paragraph yourselves, but OK, let's do it.

Bear in mind one thing. At this stage, Cooper had flirted with the idea of an act based on ineptitude but hadn't yet embraced it. He was still into the idea of being a magician. Anyway, Tommy Cooper decided, bless, to do the milk bottle trick. You know the milk bottle trick. It's the one where you turn the milk bottle upside down, take the top off and the milk stays inside the bottle.

The audience were in stitches, the audition was a success. 'I played a few shows for the troops in Cairo,' Cooper relates in his mock-biography, *Just Like That*. 'One of the most popular ditties at the time was a little number called Up Your Pipe, King Farouk, dedicated to the then-king of Egypt, which the British tommies always sang with gusto on every special occasion as a mark of respect. One of my friends, he had a smoke-curing factory in Blighty, opened up a smoke house in Cairo for smoking camel. He reckoned it would be the biggest thing since smoked salmon. He said that smoked camel sandwiches were a natural. He got the idea from an American poster he saw in Cairo which said "Smoke Camels".'

One night, Cooper was performing his act to a group of soldiers in a NAAFI club and, unbeknown to him, watching in the wings was the fickle finger of fate. One of his pieces involved using a pith helmet and, really, and you're not going to be short of a pith helmet in a NAAFI club. Most soldiers keep them neatly tucked away on their heads. This is what Tommy usually did. Not this night. He started the routine and when it got to the bit about the helmet he reached up to his head and – nothing. The helmet wasn't there. But, as chance would have it, a local waiter happened to be walking past the stage carrying a tray of drinks. Quick as a flash, Tommy reached out and took the hat off the waiter's head, put it on and used that instead. The laugh Cooper got for simply putting a fez on his head, well, no self-respecting comic was going to turn that down. It was a gift from the gods.

Useful as the fez was, there was one other useful prop that Cooper picked up during his days in the forces.

'He was in a Christmas Eve show on a boat going from Port Said to Alexandria when I first saw him,' said the woman who was then called Gwendoline Henty, 'and if people ever talk to me about love at first sight, I point to myself.' Like Tommy, she was 26. An accomplished pianist, she had been enlisted to entertain the troops. 'He was a comedian and I was a pianist. We were doing the show and I said to this huge great man, "Give me your dots." You know. "Give me your music." And he said he didn't have any music. "Just play the Sheikh Of Araby," he said. And that's how we met. He had the most magnificent physique I'd ever seen. He weighed twelve and a half stone and had these enormous shoulders. I noticed that his eyes were as blue as the sea. Even then, he was surrounded by a group of people, making them laugh. I thought he was the funniest man I'd ever seen. "This man's got star talent," I told myself. "One day, he'll be a big star."'

Tommy's telling of the story is necessarily more Tommy. 'Dove [his nickname for Gwen] was a civilian entertainer with the Combined Services Organisation and we met while doing the same show in Alexandria. She wasn't a bad-looking girl, so I sat next to her on the bus going back to headquarters. I said to her, "Can I put my head on your shoulders?"'

Ahhh, you can almost hear Cupid's arrows. Not so strangely, Cooper sorted out his relationship with meticulous speed. Two weeks later he asked Gwen, 'I suppose you wouldn't marry me, would you?'

There was a complication. When Gwendoline got on that boat to Alexandria, she was alone but not exactly single. She had been engaged to a pilot who was killed on a mission to Cologne. Her heart was still a scorched terrace – so she thought.

What would she have done if her pilot had survived?

'I'd have broken off the engagement. I really fell for Tommy.'

Two months after that first 'date' in Alexandria, they found themselves walking out of a chapel in Nicosia, Cyprus, man and wife. Their honeymoon consisted of one night in the Savoy Hotel. The Savoy Hotel, Famagusta. Just as it is supposed to be, they had not slept together before. And just as it is supposed to be, it was 'bloody wonderful'. ▮

'I was showing my wife this one. I said, "Look at this, dear." I always call her dear. She's got antlers growing out of the side of her head.'

The Perfect Double Act

'Certainly there have been times that I have known disappointment, even despair. The public never realised because I was laughing on the outside while I was crying on the inside. Very dangerous that – you could easily drown'.

A FEW MONTHS AFTER leaving the army in 1947, Tommy Cooper went full-time professional. Well, full-time when he could get the work. His television debut was on 24 December, 1947 in *The Leslie Henson Christmas Eve Party*. In terms of waiting for a break, it was no time to wait at all. But that was an early peak. Things dried up after that and he had to wait until November 1948 before his first gig, at the Collins Music Hall in Islington, north London. For the next two years, Cooper toured the smaller end of the variety theatre circuit. The period between the Henson show and the Collins Music Hall was a fairly grim time for the Coopers, and he spent more time as a barrow boy in the Portobello Road market in west London than on the stage. Picturing Cooper selling in a market, standing there, not really saying much, just standing there picking up whatever it was he was selling, looking at it, walking around a bit, putting it down, it's a wonder he didn't make a fortune. But it wasn't quite that easy, and in the real world selling handbags for twenty-five bob each wasn't much of a living. Only Tommy's self-confidence kept them going. Tommy's self-confidence and Gwen's practical get-on-with-it spirit.

An interesting character herself, Gwen

is in many ways as big as Tommy was. Loud and strong and physically imposing, she gives the impression of being one of those people whose dictionary doesn't have words like 'if' and 'but' and 'maybe' in it, that if you looked up the phrase 'Doesn't suffer fools gladly' you'd see the explanation, 'Gwen Cooper'.

Almost immediately they got together, Gwen became 'Dove'. 'Heaven knows why,' said Dove. 'Anyone less dove-like is hard to imagine.' Tommy once said that the name came because he felt all lovey-dovey when he was with her.

Gwen, solid as a rock, took any job to support them. Totally confident in her man's ability and secure in the knowledge that he would make it, Gwen provided the back-up Tommy needed.

Actually, when he left the army, Tommy wanted Gwen to get in on the act with him. Re-form the double act that had first hit the boards in Alexandria. The act then had been quite successful. 'We got together to do a comedy double act in which we had this almighty row on stage. And we were very good, too,' remembers Gwen. 'We were so convincing that when we were rehearsing in a room in Cairo, the caretaker came in and saw us slanging away and wanted to call the police.'

That was then. Now solid-as-a-rock Gwen knows better. 'I remember telling him that marriages in showbiz can easily fold up. So I told him to forget the double-act and do the magic act on his own. Then you've got no one to fall out with but yourself. Those were my exact words. And I told him that if he ever did dirty jokes or told sick stories that could hurt people, I'd divorce him.'

There's one incident from this time which sums up that post-war struggle. It was a Sunday and Tommy and Gwen were living in a furnished flat in Clapham, south London. 'Sometimes,' Tom later recalled, 'on a Sunday we'd have a walk round the West End and perhaps have half a pint of bitter each. This particular day we'd splashed out and had two halves each. Then we realised that we'd miscalculated and spent our return fare. We wandered around for a while and then Gwen had an idea. A friend from abroad had sent her a pair of nylon stockings. At the time, nylons were like gold dust. As Sunday was our big day out, naturally Gwen was wearing them. Gwen realised that the only thing we had of any value at all was her nylons, so she dived into a doorway, took them off and gave them to me with instructions to sell them.'

'I was stopped by a policeman the other day and I thought I'd have a joke with him. I had two bags with me and the policeman said, "What have you got in that bag?" and I said, "I've got some sugar for my tea," and the policeman pointed at the other bag and asked what I had in that bag and I said, "Sugar for my coffee." Then he took out his truncheon and hit me. I said, "What was that for?" And he said, "A lump for your cocoa."'

Tommy and Gwen step out in 1977.

Life with the Coopers. He kept all the props in his case and one night he was stopped by a policeman. After a bit of chat, the policeman let him go. It wasn't because he was famous, because he wasn't. It was just because he was Tommy Cooper and when the copper said 'Empty your pockets'...

Those early years set the pattern for things. Tommy creating, Gwen driving. It was a winning formula and even though their circumstances changed later in life neither saw any reason to change their roles. Later, when success had come to stay, Tommy and Gwen bought a holiday cottage away from the bright lights in Eastbourne. 'It was a wonderful hide-out,' said Gwen. 'I was born just up the road and christened just around the corner. Next door was the shop that I used to buy my gobstoppers from on the way home from school. It was the perfect place.'

Even so, when they went down there 'I was the one who had to drive there with all our stuff while he took the easy way on the train, reading scripts and having a drink. When I got there, I picked him up from the station.'

'I found this old violin and this old painting so I took them to an expert and he said, "What you've got there is a Stradivarius and a Rembrandt. Unfortunately, Stradivarius was a terrible painter and Rembrandt made rotten violins."'

'Is There Anything Else You Can Do? Anything At All?'

'If he could recapture that and channel it, we've got something that no one else is doing.'

THERE ARE A FEW SET THINGS that you need if you are going to be a showbiz success: a large slice of luck, a supportive partner, a few lumps of talent and a smart, shrewd manager. In the last few paragraphs we've ticked off all of the above except for that last vital ingredient. Then again, I suppose that if you're in possession of a large slice of luck, the smart, shrewd manager will dutifully follow. Late in 1947, Tommy met a small, grey-haired Scot called Miff Ferrie, a trombonist in a band called The Jackdaws, and everything fell into place. Well, not quite. There was still the little matter of the audition in front of Miff…

Inexplicably, Tommy chose to re-enact a scene out of *Mutiny On The Bounty* with him playing the parts of Charles Boyer and Charles Laughton. I don't know. What do you call it? Laughable or perplexing? Seeing the bumbling, shambling Cooper trying to impersonate

the dapper, sexy Boyer… Then, replacing one idiot hat with another, he became Charles Laughton. 'Mr Christian. Come down off that mast.'

Ferrie looked at Cooper.

'Is there anything else you can do? Anything at all?'

'I can do a bit of magic,' said Tommy, grinning like someone who knew what they were doing and hit Miff with ten tricks in rapid succession. He threw them at Miff like he was trying to get rid of them. Out of the ten tricks, eight collapsed around him and the quicker they collapsed, the quicker the next one followed. Miff later admitted that he didn't really know whether it was all deliberate or not. 'In a brief moment I saw this feller thinking, "Oh, my God! What am I going to do next?" and I thought to myself, "Well, if he could recapture that and channel it, we've got something that no one else is doing."'

Unsure of the nugget that the gods had dropped at his feet, Miff scratched his head. Not expecting to ever see him again, he sent Tommy on his way and suggested that he should 'work up a comedy/magic spot of about nine or ten minutes and spoil everything apart from two tricks – just to show people that you can do it.'

Two weeks later, Tommy turned up with his nine or ten minutes and nine or ten minutes later Miff signed Tommy up. When he did his second audition, even the boys in Miff's band fell about – and Miff figured, not unreasonably, that if you can make band members laugh, you can make anyone laugh.

Miff booked him to appear as the second spot comedian in a show starring Marqueeze and the Dance of the Seven Veils, a wonderfully-named music hall act that long ago sand-danced away into burlesque history.

Marqueeze and the Dance of the Seven Veils. The name alone conjures up a nostalgic picture. A small hall, the stage trimmed with a frilly curtain and lit by a row of floor lights at the front. A pit between the stage and the audience where the house band would sit and play their notes. On would come Marqueeze, following possibly a cycling act like the Wonder Wheelers, maybe Jacky the Dutch Boy, who would balance on his hands on wooden blocks, building up his pile of bricks. The tableau acts (men and women in white riding white horses with white dogs). Axe-throwers, knife-throwers, rag doll dancers, Egyptian hieroglyphic dancers, sand dancers, mechanical dancers. Speciality acts like Old Mother Riley and Kitty, illusionists like Lionel King. Tattersall, who did a speciality 'vent' act with lifesize clockwork dummies that he built himself. And, of course, Wilson, Keppel and Betty.

After these entertainments Marqueeze, make-up dripping under the heat of the lights, would perform her dance of the seven veils. Well, six veils. There would always be a little something left for audience to take home with them in their mind's eye. It's a picture straight out of fictional memories of watching Max Miller, informed by such diverse films as Laurence Olivier's *The Entertainer* and *The Night They Raided Minsky's*.

It's tempting to wonder how someone like Marqueeze must have viewed Tom. Like a young pup, eager to learn and ready to please? Or like some hot young

striker up from the reserves ready to
displace her in the first team? Probably a
mixture of the two. While artists from
Marqueeze's generation couldn't have
known what was coming – in the late
1940s, it would have taken an HG Wells
to foresee how the rise of the crackling
box that was television would change
the world – they must have been able to
sense that their world wouldn't last
forever, if only by knowing that nothing
lasts forever. Then again, I don't suppose
they thought like that at all. Who does?
Realistically, the furthest ahead they
looked was to make sure that they were
booked and that they weren't booked at
the Glasgow Empire.

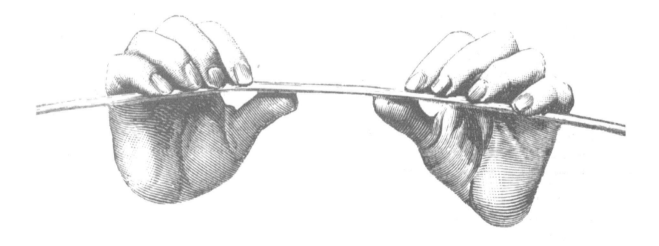

*'I was in Margate last year for
the summer season. A friend
of mine said, "You want to go
to Margate. It's good for
rheumatism." So I went there
and I got it.'*

Blue
Magic

A Gay New Glamour Rev[ue]

PRINCE OF WAL[ES]
PICCADILLY

PROGRAMME . . . . SIX PENCE

Almost a Magician

A funny thing happened on the way to the theatre...

A programme from *Blue Magic*, just one of Tommy's many bill topping shows in London's West End during the 1950s and 1960s.

AS SOON AS FERRIE TOOK CHARGE of his career, Cooper began a two-year period of hard graft, a period that included a tour of Europe and a stint in a pantomime where, curiously, he played one of the ugly sisters, and which culminated with a booking for a season at the Windmill Theatre, a place where nearly all of the wartime entertainers ended up. This was a time of work, work and work. When a performer wasn't working, they were looking for work. Competition was high and the stakes were higher. At the Windmill, Cooper doubled up doing cabarets and one week did 52 shows. One week, 52 shows. OK, so he was an ambitious, hormone raging young man in his late twenties, but that's still an astonishing amount of work.

Anyone who's ever been freelance will know the feeling. Someone asks you to do something and... what can you say? You might be working all the hours in the calendar, you might have work coming out of your ears, you might be stressed beyond stress, you might be working so hard that you're doing 52 shows in one week. But then the phone will go and an offer will come. Job 53. The freelancer cannot refuse it. What if he does? What if it's the last job that anyone ever offers him? What if that particular job is the job that is the key that unlocks the door to the future? What if he refuses that job and someone else gets it? Freelancers don't take chances and Tommy Cooper wasn't

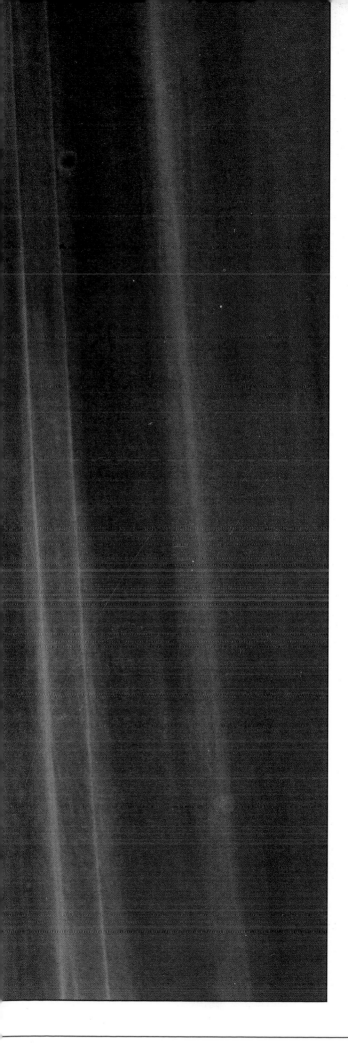

taking any chances. Not that he really had to worry. During these years he played every first-class London nightclub – and every time his booking was extended. There wasn't a club in London that didn't want him.

Ferrie booked him into the Windermere Club in Regent Street. It all sounds so romantic, doesn't it? The Windermere Club in Regent Street. A night-time world that came out to play after the normal people had gone to bed. Smoke in the air, men who looked like Laurence Harvey and women who'd get you into trouble. The Windermere Club was a place where you'd have to dress up to get in, somewhere where you'd have a table.

For the performer, the reality was a little less romantic. By the time you'd get on it would most likely be tomorrow morning, usually about 1am. The audience was, for the most part, loud and drunk and if you wanted their attention you had to go out and get it. Clinking glasses, chatter, waitresses and cigarette girls moving around, the general hubbub of people. A comic just walking out on to the stage giving it a little bit of the old 'A funny thing happened on the way to the theatre,' wouldn't last very long at all. This huge six-foot-four geezer in a dinner jacket and a fez, nervously giggling. ''Ere, have you seen this bloke on the stage? What's he all about then?'

Tommy would just stand there, absurd in this setting. And people would look at him and, regardless of who they were or what they were doing, they would laugh because, as Paul Daniels has said, Tommy emanates laughter.

From here, Ferrie got him into the

Collins Music Hall, an important showcase, neither of them looked back.

Not that everyone fell at Tom and Miff's feet. Despite being billed as 'almost a magician', the very idea of his act baffled some theatre managers. There's the story of a manager in Barnsley who complained that he'd had this turn who he booked to do a twice-nightly act for 12 nights and all the time he was there, he'd never got any of his tricks right. Yeah, OK, the manager conceded, he'd laughed at this bloke but he'd never have him back.

Remember the name of that bloke who turned down The Beatles? No, I thought not.

These were heady times and doors were opening in front of our boy before he could even get to the door handle. His act might have been all about things going wrong, but as far as the real world was concerned, Tommy was being managed by King Midas. No sooner did he appear on one stage than a bigger one beckoned, which I suppose is both fair enough and reassuring. After all, we'd all like to think that we live in a meritocracy where talent will win. Tommy's post-war career seemed to personify this idea.

He appeared at the London Hippodrome in a show called *Encore Des Follies* for its entire run from 1951 to 1952. After that, he got his big break on the all-important telly when he starred in the BBC series *It's Magic*, a show that played every fortnight from 12 March to 19 June 1952. He made his debut on the stage of the London Palladium — a key moment for any post-war performer — in July 1952. After that came more cabaret and then his first tour for the all-

important Moss Empire circuit where he was booked as one of the bill-toppers.

In 1953, there was a revue called *The Peep Show Revue Tour*. It's sweet, isn't it? *The Peep Show Revue Tour*. This is nearly half a century ago and what's changed? Nothing's changed. Then, as now, if you want to catch people's attention sling in a title like that and wait for the bookings to roll in. At the *Peep Show*, Tom was allowed to be both comic and magician and, needless to say, he flourished. When the bill was being drawn up for the London Palladium for the Coronation season, Tommy's was one of the first names on the piece of paper.

'I was woken up this morning by a tap on the door. I must remember to get the plumber to take it off.'

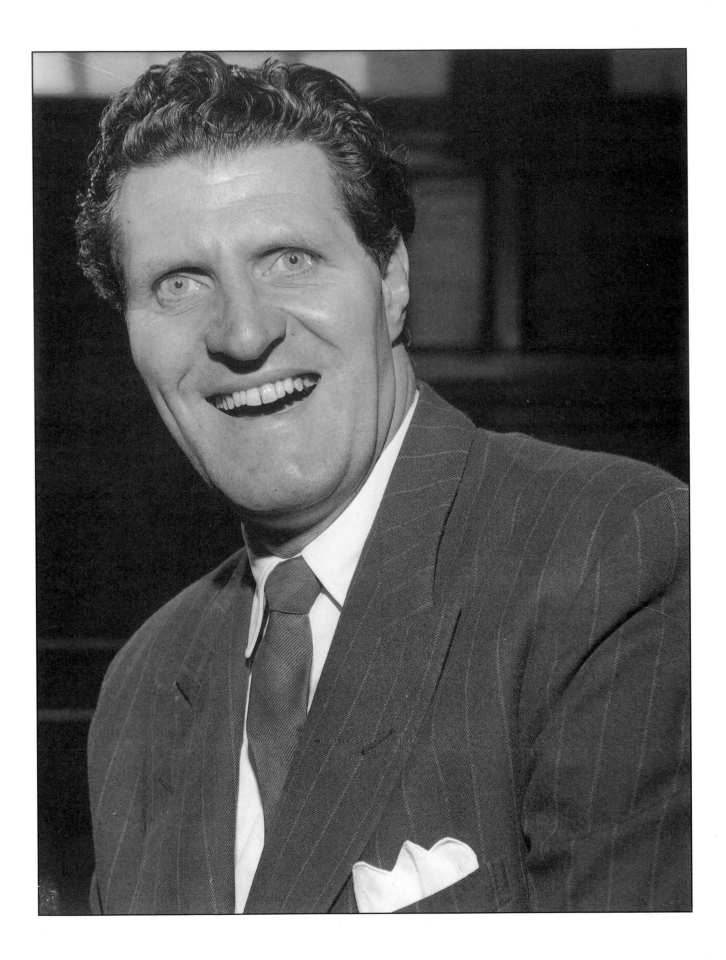

The Rat Pack and Me

Oh, the wonderful world of showbiz. From Las Vegas to the Dudley Hippodrome.

AMERICA BECKONED and the next year Tommy duly made his debut at the Hotel Flamingo in Las Vegas. Stop reading for a minute and sit down and try to picture it. The Hotel Flamingo in Las Vegas. You've got Sinatra, Dean Martin, Sammy Davis… all the boys. You've got the Mafia with their excesses, the thousands upon thousands of small-town hopefuls with their nickel and dime dreams. You've got more flickering lights than the biggest flickering light shop you can imagine, you've got neon, money and tasteless flash glitz. And Tommy Cooper, all fez and size 13 shoes, walks on stage with a pair of glasses with antlers stuck on them. 'Uh-huh. Horn-rimmed glasses.' As a visual image, I'm not sure I can think of anything more incongruous. Frank Sinatra doing My Way, Tommy doing the gag about going to see his doctor. 'I had to. He was ill.' Priceless.

It's a curious thing, though. The Americans loved him. Well, let's be a bit more specific. They loved the stuff he was doing then. The later stuff, the gags that we're more familiar with, they didn't get that at all. It was much, much too surreal. Much too Spike Milligan. Can you really image Cooper coming out to a group of sophisticate New Yorkers or a group of good ol' redneck

PRINCE OF WALES
PICCADILLY CIRCUS
6·15 TWICE NIGHTLY 8·50
VAL PARNELL AND BERNARD DELFONT
PRESENT
BENNY HILL
NEW AND EXCITING
Folies Bergère revue
By arrangement with M. PAUL DERVAL (Director, Folies Bergère Theatre, Paris) & MICHEL GYARMATHY
"PARIS BY NIGHT"
WITH A HUGE CAST ...... INCLUDING
TOMMY COOPER
30 FOLIES BERGÈRE GIRLS
Produced by DICK HURRAN

boys and doing the horn-rimmed glasses gag? If they could get past the Cooperesque pronunciation, they'd think he was taking the piss.

Back in 1954, things were different. Back in 1954, the Hotel Flamingo with its glitz loved him and so did America. On his way back to England, he stopped in New York where he was offered a season at the Radio City Music Hall. A nice offer, but he couldn't accept it. He was booked solidly for the next two years in England. Booked solidly for the next two years. What a position for a comic to be in.

Oh, the wonderful world of showbiz. From Las Vegas to New York to the Dudley Hippodrome, where he was down to play the King in *Humpty Dumpty*.

Cooper's workload in the mid-1950s was staggering. He was working and that was about it. The Garrick Theatre, Stockport. The Prince Of Wales Theatre, where he co-starred with Benny Hill in *Paris By Night* for 17 months from April 1955 to September 1956. The Coventry Theatre invited him to be the star turn for its birthday season in 1956. He played panto at the Manchester Hippodrome - the King in *Puss In Boots*. One of the reasons that Cooper could work so much was that he hadn't yet sold his soul to the telly. It's Magic apart, he hadn't really done much television and so his material hadn't been diluted by the cathode tube. Even the series It's Magic was, what? Five years earlier?

Cooper could work up and down the land, confident that he could peddle the same idiot nonsense to town after town after town. (The only place where he couldn't feel secure was the Glasgow Empire, but that was for completely

different reasons. Known as 'the graveyard of English comics', the 3,000-capacity Glasgow Empire sounds a cracking place. If you weren't English and you weren't a comic, that is. And for English comic, read Christian in Roman times.)

Tommy Cooper did do television during the mid-1950s, but, with remarkable good sense, he limited it to big spectacular showcases, things like *Saturday Showtime* and ATV's *Sunday Night At The London Palladium*. Shows like that allowed him to come on, be a star and then leave. A quick hit that reached millions, that didn't spill too much material and which established his face and name in the minds of those millions who didn't go to the clubs.

In 1957, after the panto season at Manchester, he made his first proper TV series. Made by Associated-Rediffusion, *Life With Cooper* went out live on Monday night for 12 weeks and was such a success that, even before the run was finished, the studio bosses offered him another series. Clever Tommy politely declined. He'd had enough of the telly for one year. Best get back to the roots. Best get back to where you once belonged. And that's what he did. He went back up north and back into the panto and variety circuit and the summer season at the North Pier Pavillion in Blackpool before landing back in London to play in *Robinson Crusoe* with another old hero of his, big-hearted Arthur Askey.

This was starting to look like a routine and as a routine it was hugely successful. If someone in Tommy Cooper's position had written down how he'd want his year to go, his career to go, it wouldn't have been very different. A bit of variety, his own TV series, a few big-budget television spectaculars, a high profile panto with another big name. In 1958, the TV series was *Cooper's Capers*, again for ATV, the panto was *Puss In Boots* in Bournemouth and then on to London to star on a bill with Shirley Bassey (though not, it should be said, in the panto. No, the idea of Shirl in *Puss In Boots*... I don't know. Maybe, but only as long as she was playing Puss rather than Boots.)

From here on in, life was set. The Hippodrome in Brighton (live), *Sunday Night At The Palladium* (television), *The Billy Cotton Band Show* (television), the Christmas season at the Manchester Opera House (live), the spring season at the Coventry Theatre (live), the summer season at the Princess Theatre, Torquay with Morecambe and Wise (live), the autumn season in Manchester (live). Then onto panto at the Alhambra in Bradford.

Throughout much of this time Cooper was performing while enduring a slipped disc. He went on to fulfil a twenty-week season in Blackpool before finally taking some time off for some oesteopathic treatment, but, true to form, he then flew to Aden to entertain the troops before going straight into Panto in Manchester.

March 1963 and Tommy went across the water again to do a couple of appearances on *The Ed Sullivan Show*. It's interesting to note that Ed Sullivan, who could make or break acts without stopping for breakfast, took a shine to Tom. On the second show, Mr Ed introduced Tommy as 'the funniest man to ever appear on this stage'. As the words came out of his mouth, someone put a rocket under Tommy's size 13s and

his career went 'whoosh' again.

A summer season at the Pavilion Theatre in Bournemouth (live), *Sunday Night At The Palladium* (television), the London Palladium summer show (live), the panto at the Golders Green Hippodrome (live), cabaret at the Blackpool Queens Theatre (live). Then it was time for a bit of telly and in February 1966 he started another series called *Cooperama* for ABC. A runaway hit, it was quickly followed by more of *Life With Cooper*.

He would have been a natural during the era of silent comedies, and what he said always seemed to act as a secondary line of offence, reinforcing the impact that his ridiculous physical image had made. His speech, that rough-hewn Cooper noise, was a kind of desperate gabble that got increasingly desperate as his gags and tricks continued to go wrong, his catchphrase 'Just like that' imploring the trick to go the way it was 'supposed' to. ▉

At the 1964 Royal Command Show, he walked onstage with a heater. 'They told me to go out and warm the crowd up.'

A programme (right) from one of Tommy's many performances of *Puss-In-Boots*. This one at the Alhambra in Bradford.

ALHAMBRA THEATRE
BRADFORD
GWLADYS STANLEY
LAIDLER
PRESENTS—
S. H. NEWSOME'S
Puss-in-Boots
PROGRAMME

TOMMY COOPER

Freak or Unique?

'What made him unique was his dexterity. He only had one predecessor and that was W C Fields. He was a brilliantly accomplished juggler but on stage he would literally throw it all away, and once it started going wrong the audience would be in on it, which is always the great secret of a focused performer. The audience will only love a performer who lets them in.'

– Clive James

IT SHOULD BE NOTED THAT, while what everyone says about there only being one Tommy Cooper is true and, yes, they threw away the mould when they made him and, yes, they'll never be another one like him, while I'm not criticising Tommy or saying that he wasn't an original - because he was - Tommy wasn't without precedent. As long as there'd been the music halls, there'd been comedy magicians, people like the tall, gangly Donald B Stewart. People like Len Gazeka, an obscure pre-war Midlands club comic. Gazeka used to come on stage with a 'magic' carpet and unroll it. When he was standing on the carpet, his magic tricks would work. When he wasn't standing on the carpet? Guess.

There was an American comedy magician who Tommy always made a point of seeing whenever he played London. The Amazing Mr Ballantine used many of the gags and props which Tommy appropriated and which have since been associated with him. The crap gags. The idiot props, like the arrow through the head. The cup and ball, which Tommy adopted as a running gag. You know, you catch the ball in the cup, only you never do because the ball won't go in the cup. Another one involved putting some eggs on a board which sat on top of a row of glasses. You whip the board away and… sometimes they fell in. Not often, though. The other comedian that Tommy felt a great affinity for was another music hall stalwart, Monsewer Eddie Gray. A wonderful character and a member of the Crazy Gang, Gray lived in the same idiot world as Cooper.

'Doctor, doctor. It hurts when I do that.'

'Well, don't do that then.'

Gray would have appreciated that. The Monsewer also had a penchant for performing conjuring tricks that, somehow, didn't quite work as he hoped. Curiously, though, he too was an exceptionally gifted magician. But it's perhaps unfair to point all this out. The halls at that time were full of acts that had a little bit of this one and a little bit of that one. People borrowed gags all the time. It's just that sometimes they forgot to give them back.

The other thing about the music halls is that, in many ways, they were incredibly crass and basic. The gags that drifted around the circuit were for the most part the idiot puns and ridiculous logic-defying stupidity that we've come to associate with Cooper.

Wrong time, wrong place. There's no use being the most gifted comic of your day if your day is a day when comedians are out of fashion. As everyone knows, the thing about comedians - and this is especially true of comedy magicians - is that timing is everything. You've got to have the gift of micro-timing - which enables you to do your act - and you've got to be blessed with macro-timing - which means that you appear at the right time. Those other comedians, they didn't have it and Tommy Cooper did. And that's the end of the story. ◼

'I take my drinks neat. But sometimes I let my shirt tail hang out a bit.'

Cooper, a Film Star?

Tommy made a number of small British films in the late '50s and early '60s. Among them *And The Same To You* in 1960.

According to publicity material from long ago Tommy played 'Horace Hawkins, a punchy-drunk, dim-witted pugilist.' Whatever, he found himself in the company of Brian Rix and Sid James amongst others but looks like he didn't get to kiss the girls much.

The screenplay for the film was based on the play, *The Chigwell Chicken*. No, really, it's true.

WEDNESDAY MARCH

PERCY GIBBONS
v
CHAPPY TUCK

JEN LEECE	DAI DINK
HARRY HANNEY	LES HYNNE
JACK MINSKI	MIKE MACKAY
HENI PASMORE	JO POLLOCK
BILL BENNISON	JAKE JONES
HORACE HAWKINS	BILL PINNS

DON'T MISS

BRIAN RIX · TOMMY COOPER
VERA DAY · LEO FRANKLYN
TONY WRIGHT · RENEE HOUSTON
DICK BENTLEY · JOHN ROBINSON

"AND THE SAME TO YOU"

ALSO STARRING
WILLIAM HARTNELL · SIDNEY JAMES

Tommy Cooper

In 1963 Tommy starred in *The Cool Mikado* along with a bevy of other British variety stars of the time including Frankie Howerd, Mike and Bernie Winters, Lionel Blair and, from the USA, Stubby Kaye. Interestingly, this was one of the earliest feature films made by British director Michael Winner, The script was adapted from the Gilbert and Sullivan opera *The Mikado*, but cooler, obviously.

HAROLD BAIM
presents

FRANKIE HOWERD

TOMMY COOPER

DENNIS PRICE

JACQUELINE JONES

MIKE & BERNIE WINTERS

LIONEL BLAIR AND HIS DANCERS

KEVIN SCOTT

and STUBBY KAYE

The Craziest

Adapted from the Gilbert & Sullivan opera "The Mikado" by MAURICE BROWNING   Written and

The Whackiest

The Maddest

...cal Ever Filmed!

COOL KADO

...l by MICHAEL WINNER   Produced by HAROLD BAIM   EASTMAN COLOUR

Michael Winner, complete with director's viewfinder around his neck, talks with Frankie and Tommy on set (right). Wonder who had the last word?

Top of the World

'He said, "I was acting." I said, "If I'd have wanted an actor, Tom, I'd have got one.'

– Eric Sykes

NOT SURPRISINGLY, given his love of the visual, another of Tommy's heroes was the French comic Jacques Tati, and Tommy had long nursed a desire to make Tati-esque films, silent movies that slipped between slapstick and the surreal – and is there much of a difference? Slapstick has, unfortunately, acquired a reputation as the humour of the stupid, but it's not that simple. What would you call, for example, Spike Milligan's work? Surreal or slapstick? Most people would label it 'surreal' but that's only so that they can justify it intellectually. In truth, take away Milligan's maniacal grin and replace it with, say, Benny Hill's idiot leer and what's the difference? Both relied on visual gags, both fell down a lot and, yes, both used semi-clad women to get cheap, instant laughs. Milligan, though, had a reputation as a genius while Hill had a reputation as a smutty schoolboy. Anyway…

As it turned out, Cooper had only one opportunity to act in that type of film. In February 1967, he filmed Eric Sykes' classic *The Plank*, a 54-minute near-silent with Jimmy Edwards and Derryck Guyler. Sykes and Cooper had long been best mates, but working with Sykes was still a genuine treat. Sykes is one of those classic figures who exist in every field: the supreme professional recognised as the king by those in the business but someone who is often overlooked by the general public. Sykes was not a great showman, he wasn't a man to go out and court the press and put his name forward. He was just a very fine manipulator of the comedic art. The television shows that he made throughout the 1960s and 1970s (called, simply, *Sykes*) were classically subversive – so straight that they looked like a suburban *Terry And June*-type sitcom, yet with a twist of lemon that made them take that crucial half-step to the left. (If it didn't sound so pompous, I'd say something like 'and one day Sykes's time will come'. The thing is, one day it will. Probably the day after he dies. Still.)

'We were like brothers, Tom and I,' Sykes says. 'We met in about 1948 and though I'd never seen his act we used to meet frequently in The Clachan, a pub just behind The Palladium. We used to meet there about ten or ten-thirty and we used to walk down to a little nightclub called The Bag O'Nails. We used to stop and have a sandwich and then go on to The Bag O'Nails and I used to leave him at the door.

'He knew me because I was at that time quite well known as a writer. I used to write all Frankie Howerd's material, and Max Bygraves, Alfred Marks, people like that. I didn't write for Tom. We just knew each other. We took a shine to each other and it was a rather strange happening. Then I didn't see him for a few years because he went off to play the clubs up north. But then he came back and he used to come into my office and by this time he was the real Tommy Cooper, the Tommy Cooper you'd recognise. He would come and see me when I was out on tour and I'd go and see him in his nightclub act and he was absolutely brilliant.

'When I got the original idea for *The Plank* I was talking to Peter Sellers about it and he said that it was the funniest

thing he'd read and he'd love to do it. By the time I got it all fixed up, he was off working on another film and I had to come up with a replacement. I thought that the ideal person was Tom. It turned out to be one of those lucky choices because, as much as I admired Peter and I think Peter was a genius, I don't think he would have been, for my money, in the same class as Tom.

'There was one scene I was directing and I just wanted Tom to walk down the street towards the camera looking for the plank. That's all he had to do. I said to the crew, "Don't film this one," and I shouted "Action, Tom!" He came 'round the corner and did a lot of, you know, comic looking and what have you. He was coming towards us and I shouted, "Cut!" Of course, we hadn't filmed this but I didn't tell him that. So I said, "That's great, Tom. Now we'll do another one, just for insurance. Another take for insurance." I took him aside and said, "Just walk down the street and look as if you're being normal. Not Tommy Cooper the comic, just normal Tommy Cooper looking for that plank. I don't want anything else." He said, "I was acting." I said, "If I'd have wanted an actor, Tom, I'd have got one. So just walk down the street." So he did it, he just walked toward the camera. At the end he said to me, "Do you think that's funny?" I said, "I think that's hilarious."

'Like all great comics, he was funny being himself. If he had to tell you he was going into hospital for a life-saving operation you had to laugh, first of all because it would be the way he'd tell it, and that is the great thing about all great comics – they're funny people.'

The Plank was a huge success. Cooper

was great in it. Cooper and Sykes were great mates. Why, I can hear you ask, did they not work more together? Back to Eric: 'The Plank gave Tom a really big break and he wasn't doing any conjuring or any comedy, it was as an actor. Now this didn't please his agent and his agent tried to talk tough to me on the phone and said that if there's anything that I wanted to say to Tom in the future I would have to speak to him first. I said that was ridiculous. I said, "Tom's a great friend of mine. I'm not going to phone you before I phone my friend and naturally when we get together we talk about business and ideas and things like that. We both agreed that that he liked it and that he wanted to do it and that was it." It was just that his manager wanted to hold him close to his chest so that he

could be the only one who had Tom, you know.

'He wasn't very good. He was really... not a very nice man. And he didn't have a very good reputation. Because I wanted Tom for several other things and Tom insisted he did them, and Miff Ferrie would say, "Oh. You're feeding that other guy again, are you?" You've got to remember, Tom was the biggest thing in the country. It was snide of Miff to make those remarks. Anyway, Tom and I went in and did quite a few of my one-hour spectaculars for Thames but he wanted to do more and Miff stood between us. How he did it – and I didn't find this out until it was too late – was by saying, "Well, I'm quite happy for Tom to do this but we want so much," and the figures he was asking – it was silly money. Therefore, they said that they couldn't afford it and said that Tom wasn't available.

'Don't forget that Tom was Miff's bread and butter – not bread and butter, he was bloody cake and crumpets. You'd have thought that if Tommy was in more shows, he'd get bigger and more popular and he'd earn more and therefore Miff would earn more. That's what you'd think. I can't really go into it, but there's ways and ways of making money… Tom knew that these things happened, but it would have been nice for him to get most of it, you know.'

After a season at the swank, big-buck Mandarin Hotel in Hong Kong, Tommy came back to England to play top of the bill on ATV's *Sunday Night At the London Palladium*. Twenty years after he left the army, Tommy Cooper was at the very top of his profession. Topping the bill at the prestigious Palladium; the lucrative seaside resorts were falling over themselves to book him in for their summer and winter seasons; television producers were ringing up Miff Ferrie, offering this and that. If Cooper had written the book himself, he couldn't have improved the scenario.

And so they said 'Yes.' A summer season at the Bournemouth Winter Gardens, which broke all box office records. More appearences on *The Ed Sullivan Show* in New York. His own TV series called *Life With Cooper* began in 1967. Another TV series called *Cooper Classics*. Another TV series called *Cooper At Large*. Record-breaking summer seasons at Blackpool and Scarborough, 1969 TV Personality of the Year. And that was the 1960s. The public couldn't get enough of the boy. While the world was going psychedelic and life was all mini cars and mini skirts,

Tommy Cooper kept on going and kept on getting bigger and bigger. He might have made a concession to the new age, he might have taken some of the changes on board but if he did he did it very quietly and at home.

As the decade changed and England prepared itself for the glam-rock explosion, Tommy Cooper returned to his natural constituency and went back to lie work with a vengeance. From 1970 to 1973, he did no telly to speak of at all. Talking about his reasons, he said simply, 'I love live shows. I love an audience. Maybe that's why I sometimes stay away from television for so long.' In the same conversation, he gave a hint of what went on under the fez. 'The only show that I hate is a Christmas Eve show.' (Which is ironic, seeing that his big TV break was on *The Leslie Henson Christmas Eve Show* in 1947 and that he met his wife doing a Christmas Eve show in Alexandria the year before. Anyway.) 'There they all are, the public, sitting down in funny hats and blowing squeakers and waiting for the balloons to come down. Like a while back I did a hotel and I went on and came off and it was so noisy I could have phoned the act in. Afterwards, I was in the dressing room and a fellow came in and said "Hello, Tommy. Are you on tonight?" But I just do it for my art, you see.'

'Two tourists were standing looking at a waxwork model in Madame Tussaud's. A commissionaire came up and said, "Please keep moving – we're taking stock today."'

The Wake Up Call

'Doctor, It Hurts When I Put My Arm in the Air. Can You Help Me?'

STRESS IS ONE OF THE MOST commonly over-used words in the language. You get a headache, it's stress. Your skin starts to show signs of wear and tear. Stress. You sneeze. In the old days, if you'd have sneezed, people would have said, 'Oh, you've got a cold coming on.' Now, if you sneeze it's because you're run-down because you're stressed. Back in the 1960s – I say that as though it was a different age and in some ways it was – back in the 1960s, people didn't talk about stress so much. If someone mentioned stress, most likely they were trying to make you understand something. Back then, if you had a headache, if your skin started to show signs of wear and tear, if you sneezed you took a pill and got on with it. And then it got worse. And then it got worse, until one day you got a tap on the shoulder.

For someone working as hard as Tommy was, for someone who thought of adrenaline as a stage assistant and who lived for 'the buzz', it was no surprise. The wake-up call came in the 1968 season at Brighton Winter Gardens. When the season finished, he went into hospital for a leg operation. Tommy's legs were legendary in the business. Relatively skinny and riddled with painful varicose veins they were (no disrespect) ridiculously inadequate for his huge bulking body. He also suffered from phlebitis, a painful illness which meant he had to wear a surgical stocking, and life – or stress – finally insisted that he do something about it.

He convalesced until November, which, all things considered, was about as good as it was ever going to get. He was a showman, a performer, and there were things that had to be done. Shows that had to be played. He filmed another series of *Life With Cooper* for Thames, who would take all they could. By this time, Cooper was one of the cornerstones of their schedule, a ratings winner they could rely on. So the game started again. But Tommy was increasingly dissatisfied with the shows.

Crammed with sketches and situation comedy, they relied less and less on Tommy Cooper doing Tommy Cooper than on Cooper as a TV personality. But still, that was life this was the way that life was like. You couldn't do stand-up after stand-up after stand-up. Despite the gag that all he did was to regurgitate his old gags, it wasn't really like that. How much material would you need for a twelve-half-hour series?

Meanwhile, Tommy Cooper got back on the treadmill. A season at the Savoy Hotel. Another series of *Life With Cooper*. Another series for London Weekend Television. Summer at the Princess Theatre, Torquay. Winter at the Coventry Theatre. At the turn of the decade, he was in the London Palladium summer show for a 23 week run. In 1971, he was in the Royal Variety Performance. Spring was in Oxford, winter in Margate, summer in Skegness.

And this was the pattern. It was an astonishingly gruelling schedule and a remarkable one for someone who's act was, essentially, a one-trick pony. How many people could there have been who didn't know his act? How many people could there have been who didn't know that the trick wasn't going to work, who hadn't heard the idiot joke about the man who goes to the doctor.

'Doctor, it hurts when I put my arm in the air. Can you help me?'

'Yes. Don't put your arm in the air.'

Yet it didn't matter. People went anyway. They went and they laughed.

'A man walked into a bar. It was an iron bar.'

Princess Theatre

TORQUAY

A TORBAY THEATRE

Life with Cooper

'We're a very united family. Don't think we don't row, because we do. And when we do row, I have a real go. So does he. But he's always made me laugh and we always end up laughing like mad. He always tries out his material on me and I give him constructive criticism. Why? Because I want to eat.'

– Gwen Cooper

IT'S A CURIOUS THING that one of Tommy's most successful TV series should be called *Life With Cooper* because the Cooper household, if the stories are to be believed, sounds the sort of place that, if you weren't tuned into the same radio station, could drive you mad. One journalist recalls going round to the Cooper household and sitting there interviewing Tommy and Gwen when a scream came from upstairs. It turned out that the cleaner had found a 'severed hand' in the laundry basket. Gwen's laughter turned to shock when she discovered the 'beetle' that Tommy had put in her lap when she was off-guard laughing at the cleaner.

There's an old Jewish joke that, loosely translated, goes like this:

Man: 'My wife and I both know where we stand. I make all the important decisions – whether we should invade Iraq, when to join the ERM, what to do about Ireland – and my wife makes all the small decisions – where we should live, where to send the kids to school, what we're going to eat.'

That was Tommy and Gwen's marriage - except that she made all the important decisions, too. They had one of those 'partnership' marriages where both parties know exactly what their role is and both get on with it. Gwen's role was sorting out the finances, keeping the house, cooking the food, making Tommy as many raspberry

sponges he could eat. Tommy's role was being Tommy Cooper.

A devoted family man, Tommy doted on his kids, so much so that he took his son Thomas into the family business as his manager and assistant. 'My sister Vicky and I would always go to him for advice about our careers, friends, money – even our love lives,' said his son, Thomas. 'We kept nothing from him and his advice was always right. Unlike some showbiz dads, he was always around. He'd travel the length of the country to be with us on Sunday.'

There was something else about Tommy and Gwen's marriage: they were both big people and they both had what you might call a bit of a temper. You know the phrase 'back down'? They didn't. 'They had some colossal fights. It was usually all over in a minute, but a lot of things could be shouted and thrown around in that time – usually by my mum. She has a terrible temper and dad would spend all his time ducking, saying "All right, all right, sorry. Let's go out for a drink."' This is the woman Tommy called Dove. Maybe he did have a streak of cynicism running through him. 'But it never came to anything because he always made mum laugh. Their rows nearly always happened because he was late for everything, and she has always been a stickler for punctuality. He'd leave her fuming somewhere after promising to pick her up. Or he'd arrive home late to find another burnt dinner. That would be the cue for us kids to get out of the way. But he never upset her on purpose. He once said to me, "I try so hard to be on time, but somehow I never seem to manage it."'

The stories of Tommy and Gwen arguing are legion and legend. There was a pattern. He'd be late, she'd blow up, he'd apologise and buy her a present. There's one classic story that everyone wheels out – and claims as their own – that involves him coming back from somewhere, anywhere. Late. And that night, they were supposed to have gone out. Gwen was furious and she was waiting for Tom with the mother of all tempers brewing up. Now, Tom knew what was coming – he often did. It as just that he was powerless to stop it – and he'd made provision by buying her a clock, a beautiful musical clock. So Tommy got home and opened the door and Gwen was waiting for him, all guns blazing. Apologising, Tom gives her the clock and says that he's sorry he's late – here, this is for you. Gwen takes the clock out of its box, looks at it, and hurls it across the room at Tommy. He ducks out of the way, the clock hits the wall behind him and starts playing There's No Place Like Home. Tommy and Gwen both crack up and collapse.

'The other night I dreamed I was eating a huge marshmallow. When I woke up, the pillow was missing.'

Planet Cooper

'He never had any idea of time. His timing was absolutely brilliant, but time itself meant nothing to him.'

— Jimmy Tarbuck

PART OF THE LEGEND of Tommy Cooper was his punctuality. On Planet Cooper, time had the same sort of relationship as gravity has on the moon. It might have been there, but if it was, it was hiding. The big man had no idea, which was unfortunate because both his wife and his best mate were sticklers — for sticklers, read fanatics — about punctuality. If he had a row with Gwen, odds-on it was to do with time. If he had a row with Sykes, odds on it was to do with time.

Time and again, they'd argue about it.

'He used to call rehearsals at 11am and "hope" that he'd get there for two,' said Dennis Kirkland. 'Then two would come and go and you'd find that he was in the pub next door. So you'd have to send someone in there to get him and then they wouldn't come back, so you'd have to go in there and you'd end up there sitting in the pub with him.'

So you'd end up rehearsing in the pub?

'We've done that before. We used to rent a room above The Angler, the pub next to Teddington Studios, to do that. Tommy never understood the concept of time — but you got used to it. You just had to smile. You forgave him everything because he was so gorgeous.'

Picture Tommy Cooper. Picture trying to have a go at him.

Sykes's story: 'We were doing a show together and I agreed to meet Tom and the producer in a little pub at noon, to discuss ideas. Well, at noon there's no one there and, slowly, it's starting to fill up. By 12.15, Tom still hadn't turned up and I didn't know what to say, because Tom knew that I liked people to be on time. So I said to the producer, "Look. I'm going to say something to Tom when he turns up," and the producer says, "You can't say anything, it's just Tom," but then it gets to 12.45 and the pub's practically full and Tom must have got the vibe of how I was feeling because he knew that I liked punctuality. Anyway, the door flew open and standing there in the doorway was Tom wearing pyjamas and a bowler hat and he walked up to our table, looked at us and said, "I'm sorry. I couldn't get up.'"

Kirkland's story: 'We were doing a show and I arranged for rehearsals at 10am and I said to Tommy, "Now, don't be late. Promise me you won't be late." I was a bit worried about it because Eric Sykes was also supposed to be there. Anyway, Eric got on my case and said that he was concerned about Tom, concerned that he'd be there on time. And I said to Eric, "Don't worry. I've got it all sorted out. Trust me on this one." I ordered a cab to be outside his house at 8.30am. You can tell we were working with Eric Sykes because we had a script. 'Anyway, 10am came and, of course, Tommy's not there and Eric's looking daggers at me. I'm worried at this stage because, remember, we ordered a car for him. I didn't know where he was. Ten-thirty came and went and everyone's getting very irritated. Eventually, it got to about a quarter to eleven and, just as everyone's at boiling point, the door opens and Tom walks in, in his pyjamas. "I'm sorry I'm late," he said. "I couldn't get up."

'I found out later that he'd been waiting at the top of the road for nearly an hour in his cab, watching us all going in, waiting for the perfect moment to make his entrance. Then he got out of the car and changed into his pyjamas in the street. What are you going to say? That's why we loved him. So he was late, but he was perfectly late.'

OK, it's a cute story, but the interesting thing is this. There's Tom, hiding at the top of the road, sniggering to himself like a six-foot-four schoolboy with his pyjamas in his bag and he's waiting for the perfect moment. Yet he has absolutely no idea that he's really pissing off people he really loves and cares about. It just didn't occur to him. Everything was obliterated by the chance of pulling off a stupid gag. ▪

'A woman told her doctor, "I've got a bad back." The doctor said, "It's old age." The woman said, "I want a second opinion." The doctor said, "OK. You're ugly as well."'

The Saint.
Uh-huh-huh-huh.

'If you listen carefully to some of the old tapes you can hear the crew laughing. That's the mark of a funny man.'

– Roy Addison
Thames TV publicist

ROWS ASIDE, 'life with Cooper' was like living in a joke shop. Everything you touched was a gag. That soap in the bathroom? It'll make your face black. That egg in the fridge? It bounces. That tin on the kitchen table? 'I remember coming down one morning and finding a cocoa tin on the table,' said Gwen. 'I asked him what it was doing there. "I don't know," he said. I don't know why, but I believed him. I lifted the tin up, the lid flew off and a toy snake jumped out.'

I don't know. There are two schools of thought. One says that there is The One out there, your soulmate. The one that you are supposed to be with through time and for ever. The other school says that there are any number of people that you could end up with and how it turns out is a roll of the dice. I don't suppose we'll ever know the cosmic workings of the universe, but this much is true. For Tommy and Gwen to have ended up together, that was the work of the angels. 'I lifted the tin up, the lid flew off and a toy snake jumped out.' How many people would have stood for that?

'I remember once we had an American staying with us who used chimps in his act and Tommy couldn't resist it. He turned up at a home for unmarried mothers near us with a bundle wrapped in a shawl. A woman at the door welcomed him and sighed, "Not more children, not more children." Tommy pushed the bundle into her arms and out popped a baby chimp. I thought the woman was going to faint. Then I heard Tommy laughing. You could hear that laugh a mile away, and soon everyone was laughing. Even the dog treats his juicy-looking bones with suspicion. He's had too many years of sinking his teeth into rubber bones, or chasing pieces of meat tied to an invisible thread.

'We always laughed. I think I was his best friend. He'd always say to me, "Never a day

goes by without you making me laugh." He was so generous to me. Spoiled me rotten, he did. But he'd say, "If you can't have a row now or again one of you is unnecessary." We liked to have a scream from time to time, but it was never meant nastily. It was a wonderful, extraordinary marriage. I've been very privileged.'

Outside the family - and, of course, away from the stage – Tommy Cooper just got on with it. As he himself said, 'I'm just a fiend for magic. It's like some people become golf fiends or tennis fiends. Well, I'm a magic fiend. Magic is my hobby. I love doing pocket-tricks. Wherever I am in the world I got to the nearest magic shop to see what they've got. I practice wherever I am, in the bathroom or in the car. I can sit for hours, just practising.' And that's what he did. He did magic. He didn't do pro-celebrity golf, he wasn't on the Rich Smug Entertainers For Charity golf circuit, he never bothered himself with unnecessary peripherals. He did magic.

I asked Dennis Kirkland what Tommy did. 'What was life like away from stage? It was hotel rooms, like them all. Magic was his interest, comedy was his interest. He was always on tour, he was constantly on tour so he was constantly in a hotel room.'

To some people that made him a bit of an oddity. He always looked like a man who lived in his own universe, that he didn't want to sink a few at the 18th. Mind you, if the opportunity came to sink a few at the 19th, that would have been a different thing. Cooper was, at heart, his own man. 'He wasn't a shy man as some people thought,' said Gwen. 'He always got on tremendously well with people because they all loved him. But he was a bit of a loner, you know, and he'd go off into his own little world thinking about

tricks and props and things. Rather than go out with the boys, he loved to come home and disappear into his study to work on some new trick. He just lived and died for his act. He'd get everyone at it, running around for him, carving up lumps of wood for some new stunt that he had in mind.'

Even when he was away, even when he was in places where you or I might feel like, well, maybe a bit of a cavort, Tommy Cooper did magic.

Gwen: 'I remember when we went to New York a few years ago. As soon as we got out of the airport, he went off to look at a joke shop that he knew and completely forgot where we were staying. He was "lost" for seven hours and I was worried sick, but then he just sauntered into the hotel room and said that he'd been to the joke shop, hoping that I'd not noticed how long he'd been gone. I then found out that he'd phoned the family home in Chiswick to find out which hotel we were staying at.'

'I carry so many tricks and props around with me, it's like a small circus,' he once said. 'That's why I always have two rooms in a hotel. I use the sitting room as the practice room. I love what I'm doing, so when I try something new and it goes well, that's a great tonic for me. It's what I'm most concerned about.'

He showed no interest in politics. He wept openly at films about love stories. He was an insomniac who stayed up into the early hours. And what did he do in those long, lonely lost hours? He practised his latest tricks to another degree of perfection. And that was it.

Maybe that was why it came as such a shock to everyone when, just after he died, the story surfaced about the mistress that he'd had for 17 years.

'Whaaa???'

'Are you OK now? Have you picked yourself up? Yes, I did say that Tommy Cooper had had a mistress for 17 years.'

'I know, I know. How did he do that?

'Just like that.'

'Yes, yes. Very funny.'

'Is it true? This is Tommy Cooper we're talking about. Are you serious? This is Tommy Cooper.'

'Listen, I don't know the truth for nothing. The story is that he had a mistress for 17 years. Whether it's true, well that depends on who you ask, doesn't it? Anyway, where were we?'

Cooper was never interested in material things. He never owned a Rolls Royce and he never had a number plate with TOMMY 1 or perhaps FEZ 1 – what sort of showbiz personality was he? I thought it was in their contracts to have a Roller and a self-satisfied number plate. His most expensive car was a Mercedes, which, OK, isn't a beat-up Ford Escort, but still, it was over 10 years old when he died. No wonder he never got to present an idiotic ITV game show where the winner plays his cards right and takes it all. Maybe it just wasn't that important.

His great indulgence – and this is lovely – was expensive clothes. He loved clothes and, deep down, dreamed of being an immaculate smoothie like Cary Grant – who, incidentally, thought Cooper was great and sought him out whenever he could. One of the oddest couples I could conceive of, the two became firm friends and went out drinking together whenever they were in the same neck of the woods. Cooper's other great sartorial hero was his old mate Roger Moore and – this is another great mental image – fantasised about himself as Moore's character

The Saint, purely for the clothes, you understand. Tommy Cooper as the suave, sophisticated Simon Templar. You figure it out.

Maybe it's just a question of everyone wanting what they can't have, everyone wanting to be someone else. Maybe while Cooper pictured himself as Cary Grant out romancing Grace Kelly just like that, Roger Moore was standing in front of his bedroom mirror with a rose and a vase. 'A rose, a rose. A risen. Uh-huh-huh-huh.'

In his pursuit of this dream, Cooper even went to Moore's tailor and had some suits made. He went to all the best tailors and spared no expense. Shoes, too. He wore immaculate, hand-made shoes that, on anyone else, would have looked lovely. Unfortunately, Cooper had huge size 13 feet and it didn't matter how elegant his shoes were, as soon as he put them on it looked as though he were going to for a trek across a snow-covered field. Eric Sykes used to say that you could put Tommy in a £1,000 suit and he'd look like he just got out of bed.

Life with Cooper. Right up to the end, the games went on. Gwen: 'Even after 36 years of marriage I still haven't learned. I can't touch anything in this house - it's full of Tommy's tricks and props. I pick up a sauce bottle and it breaks in half. I take an egg from the cupboard and go to crack it and it bounces away because its made of rubber. I go into the bathroom to wash my face and come out blacker than I was when I went in because Tommy's put some trick soap in there.' ⬛

'I slept like a log last night. I woke up in the fireplace.'

Because He Was So Gorgeous

Comic Ade Edmondson got a shock after paying £500 for Cooper's box of tricks at an auction in 1989. 'I was expecting something incredible,' he said 'but it was just full of old bits of cardboard and old socks. I've never been so disappointed.'

WHILE TOMMY COOPER'S home life was one long whoopee cushion, everything changed when he got into the studio. As is often the case with people as driven as Cooper was, the clown removed the mask as soon as the work started. 'It's showtime, folks!' Tommy would say as he got out his trusty notebook and made careful reference to everything that would go into each show. By the end of rehearsals, he knew the structure of the show inside out. He knew how long each sketch would take, how long to spend with his ridiculous gags. He even calculated how much time would be taken up by the interruption of audience laughter. Cooper would sit in the rehearsal rooms used by all the Thames comedy stars – a custom-built studio with seats and stage like a proper theatre – and run the recordings with a near-military precision. 'Look. It's my arse that's on the line. It's my show. At the end of the day, who's left holding the sodding baby? Me. That's who.'

Now, if you take that paragraph and – apart from line about the whoopee cushion – reverse absolutely everything, you'd be somewhere near the truth of what life with Cooper in the studio was like.

Life With Cooper in the studio was like

life with Cooper at home, except it was in the studio. Dennis Kirkland spent nearly a quarter of a century working with Cooper. How do you do it, Den? How do you go about working with someone as, how shall we say, individual as Tommy? 'Of course, you just get on with Tom. He's so hysterical. He's everything that everyone wants him to be. He was exactly the same off stage as he was on – lovely and hysterical – but people used to see him and just laugh. We'd walk in The Anglers [the in-house pub opposite Teddington Studios] lunchtime after rehearsal, if he ever turned up for the rehearsal, and he'd walk in through the door and the pub would start to rock with laughter. And he just walked through the door. People always used to say that about Cooper. He only had to walk on and I was laughing, but what they forget is that it took 25 years of hard work to gain that reputation.'

Why does it always come down to hard work? That's somehow so disappointing. You see the words 'comic genius' thrown around and you just hope that it's God-given and that all he's got to do is just be. Just be a comic genius. That it comes down to hard work and sweat and dedication... It's so basic. So human. So disappointing. I suppose that it was all technique, then.

'No, I don't think it's technique. I think that it's just in them. I think that comics just know which is the best way of delivering a line for them. Tommy was the worst deliverer of a line, but the best – you know what I mean? Talk about technique and Tommy wouldn't know what you were talking about. You hone an act, knowing what works and what doesn't and if that's technique then fine, but I don't think a lot of comics stop and think about it. It's called rehearsing.'

Was he good at rehearsing? 'No. Totally useless. I once did an entire show with Tommy and he was in hospital at the time when we were supposed to be rehearsing, so we went to the hospital and we did it 'round his bed. Me and my PA and Dick Hills, and we did the gig around the bed. It was an hour special and we never rehearsed it.'

So, what? You just sorted everything out and told Tom what to do? 'Not really. We worked out all the props and got it all ready... But all that is down to knowing how it works and understanding.

'The thing with Tom is that he was, in his way, an original. It's a rarity to have an original idea, but Tommy was an original, which is why everyone copied him. You're not going to find an original joke, but he was an original shape, an original voice. The different bits of him might not have been original, but the whole package was.'

A few years back, there was a television documentary about the great jazz pianist Thelonious Monk. Now, Monk was a pianist like no other, he played like no one else and even to someone who knows nothing about the mysteries of the keyboard it was clear he was different. His contemporaries talked about him finding new notes, of playing in the spaces between the chords. They said his left hand and his right hand weren't even related. Monk's appearance also marked him out as special: zoot suit, dark glasses, beret, a neckerchief above the shirt-line, sparkling painted tie - this was someone who knew exactly what he was doing. The documentary was made as if Monk was dead. He wasn't. We'd have heard – for there was no presence of the man.

Then, about two-thirds of the way through, he appeared. The interviewer asked him a question, probably something simple about Round Midnight or something. Monk listened to the question, but made no reply. Then, after a few seconds passed, he got up and very slowly stretched his arms out and started to spin around, rather like a young child would if pretending he were an aeroplane.

As an answer, it was perfect, if a little unorthodox. Words are fine if you want to have a chat or buy a meal, but how are you going to explain the workings of the artist? More to the point, why should you? By seeking to rationalise it, you must necessarily de-mystify it and - suddenly it's ordinary. What a dull process, to make the extraordinary ordinary. Where's the fun, the joy? How much better, how much more eloquent, Monk's answer was: 'Er, I don't know how I wrote Round Midnight, but here's a quick impersonation of an aeroplane.'

WORKING with Cooper: it sounds a hoot, but it sounds an exhausting hoot. He hates rehearsing, he's never there on time. He might be hiding at the top of the road waiting for everyone to get really, really pissed off, but he's not where you want him to be. It's all right to get away with that sort of thing if you're a comic genius, but how did mere mortal professionals deal with it? As with the question of time, '…You got used to it, you just had to smile,' tells Kirkland. 'You forgave him everything because he was so gorgeous,' remember?

Working with Cooper. 'Then there was …the story of the exploding dove. We were doing a show at the BBC. They didn't have a room for us to rehearse in and we needed somewhere. So they found us us this office that belonged to someone quite important but, for whatever reason, she wasn't there. It was me, Tom, Eric Sykes and Chic Murray and Tom says, "Listen, I've got this new prop, an exploding dove. You've got to have a look at it." So he cleared a space on this woman's desk and started getting this dove out of one of his bags. And after a while, he turns round in mock triumph, as if he's doing it on stage, and introduces the exploding dove. At which point there's this huge explosion. The room's filled with smoke, there are feathers everywhere. I'm looking at Sykes and Chic Murray's sitting there completely deadpan. "That could have hurt someone." Tom is running around, "Who's been messing with my props?", pretending to be all in a panic, but of course that's the gag. Anyway, this woman's desk is ruined so we switch the lights off and sneak open the door to see if anyone's around and run off down the corridor like a group of schoolboys.'

Working with Cooper. 'Then there was the time when we'd been working late,

me, Tom and Sykes. Eventually we finish, pack up and prepare to go down to the car park to get our cars. Tom makes some excuse that he's got to go back to the office and Eric and I go down and we're in the car park when this really strong torchlight covers us and Tom's hanging out a window screaming "Stop! Thief!" and me and Eric are running off like a group of naughty schoolboys.'

The key to filming Tommy Cooper – and I think even I could have told you this – was to just let him get on with it. You point the camera and you say, 'Go'. That, to me, would be logical. But not to everyone.

'THERE was a director, a top comedy director, who took over for one show and hadn't worked with him before, and he just didn't know how to deal with Tom. Now, when Tom's doing a routine, a stand-up routine, you cover him because you'll know what he's going to start on and you'll know what he's going to finish on but everything else – you don't have a clue what he'll do.'

What do you mean? You don't know how long its going to be?

'No. If it's a live thing then obviously you know, but rarcly arc shows live so you'd get Tommy to do 15 minutes and you'd cut it down because he didn't have a running order or anything conventional like that. He'd just be going through his routine and suddenly he'd stop doing what he was doing and start with a story. "I went swimming the other day," and you don't know where that's come from or where it's going to go. But you just slave on it, slave on the big shot and let him run. Your job is to keep him covered.'

If you don't know what he's going to do, would he? Would he know?

'Well, he's got a table full of props, so if he sees a daffodil he knows he's going to do the daffodil joke but if there are a selection of jokes on the table then he could do them in any order. He'll pick something up, look at it, and put it down again. Maybe he'd go back to it later, maybe he wouldn't. And he'd always be doing that, always picking things up, looking at them and putting them down again.'

Cooper was, more than anything, visual, and he was lucky that he had someone like Sykes to bounce off: 'We had more laughs together off the stage than on it,' said Sykes. 'He was such a lovely companion. We did have serious moments, but really not too many. Mainly we were out for laughs. He had such a sharp comic brain, you know. I remember one occasion I had some people in my office, there was Bobby Charlton, Sir Matt Busby, a few football people having a drink, and in walked Tom. He was always beautifully dressed, always expensively dressed, and he had this Crombie overcoat on. It was a beautiful coat, very expensive, and in walked Tom and of course everyone says hello. We were knocking back the whisky. I took Tom's coat from him, he started telling this story and I dropped his coat on the floor by his feet. Well, as Tom's going on with this tale, he picks it up and starts dusting it down and he's still telling his tale and all the time he's dusting this coat down and when he gets a laugh at the end of his anecdote, he drops the coat on the floor and joins in the laughter. Now, this is a lovely visual gag that looked like we'd worked it out between us, but of course we hadn't. But that's how sharp Tom was.

'One day when we were making *The Plank* we were all having lunch. The lighting man and the cameraman, there were a lot of people. Tom suddenly put his knife and fork down and he lay flat on the floor and everybody looked at him. After a while Tom got up and sat back down and got on with his meal. I said to him, "What do you want to do that for?" He said, "I thought I'd do something visual."'

'My feet are killing me. You know, every night when I'm lying in bed they get me round the throat like that...'

It was New Year's Eve in Joe's Bar, A Happy Mob Was There

'To make people laugh is a privilege. It's the sound of all sounds, it's the sound of life. "A joke's not funny till its been laughed at." Eric Morecambe said that. Or was it Benny? Doesn't matter. They probably got it from someone else.'

– Dennis Kirkland

WHERE DID TOMMY get his material from? The temptation is to say 'a very, very old joke book' but, really, where did he get it from? And more to the point, who would own up to writing it? Dennis Kirkland comments, 'It's like Benny Hill would say, "I steal all my own material." But Tommy had people like Dick Hills.' Together with Sid Green, Dick Hills was the man who first scripted Morecambe And Wise. In the years before they went to the BBC and started working with Eddie Braben, Hills and Green were working at the business end.

'Tommy's act was honed from little gags from everywhere. But Tom never really told jokes – I mean, he told jokes, obviously, but he told them only in his way and he was basically very, very funny. His manner was just one that encouraged laughs. Often you'll find that if you're telling a joke to a mate of yours, you'll get twice the laugh if you tell it as Tommy Cooper. But his material came out of years of experience. People used to applaud during his act because they wanted to hear all the stories they knew. So the minute he'd say, "And now I'm going to do the very famous egg-bag routine," he'd get a round of applause. They knew it, they knew what he was going to do but they could not wait for him to do it. That's what it is.'

That's reasonable enough. If you go to a concert all you want to hear are the songs that you know and love. It's one of the great ironies of life for the concert-going classes. A performer will generally play a concert because he/she/they have a new album to promote and so they'll want to play songs from that album. But the audience, they couldn't give a hang about the new album. The chances are that if they're fans they'll buy it anyway, but at the concert what they want to hear is the old favourites.

'Tom used to get a round of applause when he just put a cardboard box on the table,' said Kirkland, 'because people thought that that meant he was going to do the hat routine.'

'It was New Year's Eve in Joe's Bar,
A happy mob was there.
The bars and tables were crowded,
Lots of noise filled the air.'

The hat story was one of the cornerstones of his act, a ridiculous multi-character story in which Cooper would have a cardboard box on his magic table full of hats and tell this nonsense story, 'becoming' each different character by putting on their hat. Of course, he could never find the hat he was looking for and always ended up chasing his own tail, becoming more and more frantic before he forgot where he was and had to start again. It was typical Cooper in that it required the timing of a district nurse just so that it would look a complete shambles. Anyway.

'PEOPLE wanted him to say all the things that they knew he was going to say, but where the material came from in the first place? It came out of the air. Tom would get away with murder, he'd say things that no one else would get away with. People got bored with everyone else, but not with Tommy. People wanted to see him do what he did. You know that if he comes on with a rose and a jar you know he going to go "A rose, a rose" and then pull a string. "Arisen".

'He used to have these gags that he'd always use but they'd never get a laugh. He'd come on and say, "My feet are killing me. Every night when I get into bed, they get me round the neck." It never got a laugh. He used to say it about three times and it would never get a laugh. But it made him laugh. He had another line like that which never got a laugh about having a lighter that wouldn't go out. A ridiculous gag. It would never get a laugh.

'People laughed at the anticipation of him – but it wasn't only that. He also looked stupid. He was a lovely man, he was a real gentle giant - that's exactly what Tommy was. Big, very funny and gentle. He was a gentle bloke. There was no aggression or anything. The thing that made me laugh a lot was that, if he was telling a joke, he would put things in that were absolutely nothing to do with it, like the joke he told about the monkey walking home through the jungle. The story is that the monkey keeps getting attacked by the lion and he asks the hyena for help. That's basically the joke. But Tommy told the story and he said, "The monkey's on his way home. He takes a shortcut. He doesn't have to, but he takes a shortcut." Now that just comes out of nowhere. I don't know, but it cracked me up.'

Did he live in the same world as us?

'Oh, I hope not, Dennis says. 'No, of course he did, but he was Tommy Cooper. He was a star.' As if by way of explanation, he adds, 'I was taking my parents back to Newcastle and we went to Kings Cross station and I looked across the concourse – and I wasn't expecting him there – and I looked across and I could see Tommy. He was standing head and shoulders above everyone else and he had a Hawaiian shirt on. You know, one of those vomit-making Hawaiian shirts and cream trousers and shoes and a pair of dark glasses. He walked over and I said, "What are you dressed like that for?" He took off the dark glasses and said, "I didn't want anyone to recognise me." He was dressed like that in the middle of Kings Cross station yet he really believed that he was in disguise because of the dark glasses. He thought that

that was what I was referring to.

'If he walked in here now, everyone would stare at him. Well, of course they would. He's dead. Tommy would like that. Actually, at his funeral, with Eric Sykes and Max Bygraves and lots of lovely people, we were sitting there and the coffin's there and, of course, you can't stop it once the giggles start and we're going, "What's going to happen to the coffin?" Eric said, "The coffin's going to go off and its going to come straight back on and Anita Harris will get out in a different dress. It's a trick. Just you wait. He'll do a 20 minute spot." Because, you know, Tommy with a coffin is perfect.

A true story: Tommy Cooper was introduced to The Queen after a Royal Command show.

'Do you think I was funny?' said Tommy.

'Yes, Tommy,' said The Queen.

'You really thought I was funny?' said Tommy.

'Yes, of course I thought you were funny,' said The Queen.

'Did your mother think I was funny?' said Tommy.

'Yes, Tommy,' said The Queen. 'We both thought you were funny.'

'Do you mind if I ask you a personal question?' said Tommy.

'No,' said The Queen, 'but I might not be able to give you a full answer.'

'Do you like football?' said Tommy.

'Well, not really,' said The Queen.

'Do you mind if I have your Cup Final tickets?'

It Was TV in the Lounge with the Candlestick

Nostalgia, we know, isn't what it used to be. Neither are the comics. You'd get people standing up and they could tell you a joke. Now it's all sex and smut. I saw a comic the other night and he told this joke that was typical. 'A tightrope walker was doing his act over a gorge with a raging river below. To his surprise, what should he see coming towards him on the rope but a very attractive stunt girl. What should he do?' the comic asked the audience. 'Go back the way he came or toss himself off?'

THINGS WERE BETTER THEN. Footballers now, they don't know they've got it made. Nowadays it's all about money, isn't it? Money and advertising hair products. And call that music? It's not like it was in the days of The Beatles when a tune was a tune and you could tell the boys from the girls.

Tommy Cooper. Could it happen now? 'Tommy would come through but the question was not whether he'd come through, but what show he'd appear on,' Dennis Kirlkland explains. 'There aren't that many shows anymore with spots for people like that. Everything now is geared towards sitcoms and away from variety shows.' That's a bit of a chicken-and-egg deal, though, isn't it? If the Coopers of the world were still around, maybe there'd be the variety shows. Maybe they're not there because the acts aren't there. It's an argument. It's not a bad argument, either. Kirlkland again: 'As any of the big boys will tell you, there aren't very many clubs to work in anymore, either. We used to have dozens of them, but now? Where can you go now to have a Bob Monkhouse topping the bill or a Freddie Starr? There used to be clubs all over the place, these good big clubs but they don't work anymore.'

So is it the old story? Did TV kill the music hall star? 'Er, no. People don't go to the clubs like they used to in the old days. They're very expensive to run and there are very few artists who could pack them out now, which you need.' Hang on a minute, Dennis. You're a TV producer. It's not likely you're going to come out with 'It was TV in the lounge with the candlestick' is it?

The truth is, as they say, out there, and it's probably quite simple. Life has changed. Culture has changed. Everything has changed. I was watching an old film called *The Jolson Story* the other night, and, OK, it's very old and it depicts life in pre-war America. OK, that aside it fits the purposes of our argument like a bespoke tie. The characters were sitting around the dinner table, wondering what to do next. 'I know,' said one. 'Let's go to a nightclub.' So off they went to a nightclub. The next time we saw them they were being shown to their table by an immaculate-looking chap in a dinner suit. 'Can I get you something?' A floor-show was going on and in the far corner a big brass orchestra played.

Fast-forward that scene to the present and what would the nightclub be? The nightclub would be different. Loud, no floor-show, no big brass orchestra. Our tastes have changed, we want different things now, different forms. And TV has played an important part in that change.

It's often a nonsense to talk of The Golden Age of anything - nearly always it's a rose-tinted view, but it does seem that something happened to comedy in the last ten to fcifteen years that it cannot recover from. Kirkland opines, 'We lost the respected characters. In very quick

succession – or at least what seemed like a very quick succession – we lost Eric Morecambe, we lost Benny Hill, we lost Les Dawson, we lost Frankie Howerd, all within the space of a couple of years. *The Two Ronnies* are no longer with us, they stopped. Thank goodness they're still here, but we lost a great big chunk of heavyweight traditional comedy that people relied on. We ripped out the heart of the defence. But nobody has come through with the authority of any of those people. They just haven't done it. The world has changed and so have the comics. The Jack Dees of the world, people like that, are a different style. They might say, "No, we're not. I'm just Max Miller or I'm just Les Dawson with a different accent." But the truth is that none of them yet have the authority to command.'

Isn't that just a question of time? Isn't that just a question of them gaining 'elder statesman' status?

'Maybe you're right, but I don't think so. People like those old greats, they came from the theatre, from the halls, and that's a completely different thing. It's why sitcoms are doing so well. If you asked people who's the funniest man in the country, they'd all say David Jason. But he's not a comedian, he's an actor, but people would say, "Well, he makes me laugh more than anyone does." They've got a point, but it's not the same, is it?'

In March 1977, a Variety Club lunch at the Savoy was held in honour of Tommy's 30 years as a professional. As he got up to speak, the 400 guests each put on a fez. Cooper looked at them and, without saying a word, (except probably 'uh-huh') reached into his pocket, pulled out a fisherman's flat cap and put it on. Predictably and on cue, the place fell apart. ◼

But He Wasn't Always Intending to be Funny

THERE'S BEEN MUCH TALK of 'The Curse Of Tommy Cooper', which relates to what happened to those close to him. It's largely newspaper nonsense talk, and I dare say that we'll get on to that in due course. But, in a very different sense, there was a curse that Tommy Cooper had to endure and it was this: Tommy Cooper couldn't turn it off. He couldn't stop being Tommy Cooper. And people couldn't stop relating to him as Tommy Cooper.

Roy Addison tells a story that illustrates the point. 'There was a freebie trip we all took to Gibraltar and there was a lot of us there, comics and press people. We went on a tour of some caves and we were just walking around and we turned round the corner and there was Tommy, sitting down, gently crying. No one was expecting to see him there. We just saw him and, of course, we all fell about, but he had actually hurt his toe quite badly and it was obviously very painful.'

The telling thing in that story is not the story, it's the 'of course'. Of course they fell about. Tommy Cooper's sitting

'I don't know if he was happy or not. I don't know anyone who knew him well enough to know if he was happy – I don't know if there was anyone who knew him well enough. He was pretty much like he was on stage, either manic or melancholy, manic or lugubrious.'

– Roy Addison

down quietly crying. Of course you're going to fall about laughing. And you've got to remember that this isn't Cooper as he's appearing in your mind's eye, all dinner suit and fez and coming on with the 'Man, cave. Cave, man' stuff. This is a man on holiday.

The burden must have been enormous.

It's all very well 'emanating humour', as Paul Daniels said. It's all very well 'not questioning it, just thanking the Lord that he gave you that gift', as Eric Sykes said, but what about when you just want to sit down and have a quiet chat about whether the Euro is such a great idea and should the government join the ERM? What about when you wanted to discuss just what was the matter with Spurs with your mates? What about it? The minute you open your mouth everyone around you cracks up. You see, it's all that 'emanating humour' you're doing. Can't you turn the volume down for a couple of minutes?

Even the people closest to him were affected. It didn't matter. When Tommy Cooper just wanted to be Tommy Cooper, ordinary bloke, people still related to him as Tommy Cooper.

Dennis Kirkland: 'I had one row with him once and ended up just laughing because he was shouting at me. It was about nothing at all, like most arguments. I'd got him this suit for a show and it wasn't right - it was supposed to be short in the sleeve and it wasn't right - and he said, "It's not right and I'm not going to do it." I'd never known him do this before, I was crying with laughter, and he just looked at me and said, "I'm not talking to you anymore, you're fucking mad," and he walked away, but I was just howling. How are you going to keep a straight face when Tommy Cooper's shouting at you?'

Did Cooper get frustrated that people didn't take him seriously? 'It's difficult to say. I don't know. The difficulty is that if you're sitting in the pub talking about government policy and Tommy starts laying down the law, its difficult not to laugh at him.'

If that was someone who'd known him the best part of two decades, what was it like out there in the big wide world? Tommy Cooper. He's not the sort of bloke you can put a false beard on and hope that nobody notices. He was going to be noticed. 'He liked going out but he was always getting disturbed,' said Kirkland. 'Because of the way he was and because he was in people's living rooms, they thought that he was an old mate and when we went out people would come up and nudge him and grab him and... it was disaster. You shouldn't do that.

'We were in a pub in Hammersmith after a show - and you've got to remember that we're just having a quiet drink — and this guy came across and said, "Here, I've got a great one for you. You'll steal this one from me" – they always accused him of stealing a joke or they'd say something like, "You'll pay me some money for it" – and this guy said, "I'll tell you a joke." Now, I know what to do. Don't laugh. And this guy tell his joke and he comes to the tag line and... nothing. Tommy's got this big stony face and he turns to the guy and says, "That's a funny joke." He turned to me and said, "What do you think, Dennis?" and I said,"Yeah, that's funny." Tommy called over for Dick Hills to come over. You can feel the heat starting to rise. Now Dick's got a great stone face and Tommy gets the guy to tell Dick his joke and Dick says, "That's funny." The bloke is getting really uncomfortable by now and Tommy makes him go through the joke with someone else and eventually the bloke gets to feel so uncomfortable. And Tommy turns round to me and says, "And, anyway, I said to this bloke," and continues the conversation we were having before the bloke interrupted us.

'There was another classic way that Tommy had of getting rid of people hassling him. I remember once meeting him once in Manchester station and he's standing in the bar having a beer. So, again, this bloke comes up and it's all "Tommy Cooper! What are you doing here?" And Tom just said, "Well, everybody's got to be somewhere." But the bloke just wouldn't let it go. He kept going on about how odd it was to see Tommy Cooper there. So Tommy gave him this story about how he lived in west London and how there was a lovely

pub at the end of his road, but sometimes he just got bored with going there. "Sometimes you get bored going to same pub all the time, so I come here."'

'He just drew people's eyes in,' Dennis explains. 'He glowed warmth. You wanted to cuddle him, you know. People just wanted to put their arms round him. This great buffoon who was doing cracker jokes and stupid little magic tricks and he was the god.'

'*A man is trying to sell his dog. So he stops another man and says: "Wanna buy a dog? He's very clever. Look at this." He throws a stick into the pond and says, "Fetch that, Rover." The dog gets up on his hind legs and walks across the water and gets the stick. "That's no good to me, mate," said the man. "He can't swim."'*

The Cooper Curse: A Celestial Trade-off

IT WAS A COOL JUNE evening in 1947 and Trooper Tommy Cooper was lying in bed contemplating the past and the future, what had been and what was going to happen. For the past seven years, he'd been in the army, fighting the good fight and entertaining his fellow soldiers. Now all that was going to end. Now life was going to really start. Tomorrow he was going to be discharged by the army – a free man! – and things were going to begin in earnest. As he lay there, he repeated the words, 'I will become a star. I will become famous. I will become a success.' Over and again he repeated the words and, as he did so, a deep sleep descended over him.

'Tommy Cooper. Tommy Cooper.'

Tommy Cooper opened his eyes. A spectral light filled the room, partially blinding him. 'Who's there?' he said.

'It is I,' said the voice. 'The Angel of Light and Dark.'

'What do you want? Haven't I paid my bill?' said Cooper.

'You want to be a star, Tommy Cooper. I can give you that. Do you want my help?'

'Who are you? What are you talking about?'

'You can have anything you want, Tommy Cooper,' the voice said. 'You will be a success, the world will fall at your feet. You will be fêted as the greatest entertainer of your day. You will have the gift of laughter. You will walk into a room and people will laugh. I will give you all this. But in return, you must give me something.'

'Anything, take anything you want,' the sleeping hulk said.

'When you die, everything will fall apart. When you die, the price will be mine. Resist, Tommy Cooper, and I will place the Cooper Curse on all you touch.'

When Tommy Cooper awoke the next morning, he remembered nothing. He packed his bags, put on his demob suit and opened the door. The sun was shining.

'I wonder what today holds?' he said to no one in particular and strode out into the new dawn.

Well, it could have been like that.

Comic genius. They're two great words, aren't they? We'd all love to be comic geniuses, madcap characters who bring laughter into people's lives. People who have that gift for making people laugh – and who was it who said that laughter was the sound of life? Doesn't matter, probably everyone. Laughter is the sound of life. Without it, what life is there? And to be able to sprinkle that over people's lives – it's truly a gift from the gods.

So why is it that when you see the two words 'comic genius' you just know that they're going to be followed by some dark story, some psychosis. Drink, drugs, gambling, women, violence. Why is it that you're left with the feeling that if X didn't have his own gameshow/film career, he'd be playing cards ('higher, higher') in Broadmoor? If you're lucky, your hero gets away with 'actually he wasn't actually a very nice man' which, actually, is simply dull. Give me a good scandal any time.

Hancock, Chaplin, Sellers, W C Fields: you can take your pick. Up until a few years ago, I thought I was going to come out unscathed in all this when it came to comic heroes. What chance, for example, was there that Woody Allen would ever be accused of child abuse?

There's obviously something in the nature of the beast that compels them to push, to drive. And it's unrealistic to think that Tommy Cooper was any different – I don't mean all that sex'n'drugs stuff, I just mean that, in order for Cooper to succeed like he did, he must have been driven by a burning ambition. And despite all that bumbling around on stage, everything was all worked out to a T.

Thomas, his son, was in charge of his props and told a story that belied the shambles. 'The tables on the stage looked like a jumble sale but Dad knew where everything was, provided I did my job right, which took over an hour. And if I didn't! Once, in the middle of his act, he realised that I'd forgotten a vital prop, so he just called to me in the wings: "Tom, where are the scissors?" I walked on sheepishly with them and the crowd fell about laughing.'

Despite all the stuff about Cooper being an innocent who pandered to the child within because he was, as it were, the child without, you just know that beneath that idiot facade there lurked a perfectionist who knew exactly what he was doing and how he was doing it. While there is palpably a conspiracy of silence surrounding Cooper's his drinking – and that isn't meant in some sinister Masonic way, it's just as one of the inner Cooper clan (unnamed) said to me, 'You protect your own' – two stories came to light shortly after his death that put a chink in that shiny armour. The first occurred quite recently; the second immediately after Cooper's death.

In 1994, Garry Lyons wrote *Frankie And Tommy*, a play based on the wartime experiences of his father, Frankie Lyons, and Tommy Cooper. The picture painted is of a driven ego prepared to do anything – to anyone – to get to the top. When the play opened, Garry went on the defensive and played a straight bat – 'Tommy

Cooper was a comic genius and I hope we give him full credit for that' – but it was such a shock that someone spoke less than favourably about one of the nation's favourite icons that the play caused a furore.

The story was this. In 1946, ENSA officers thought it might be a good idea to put their two top acts together in a variety show. Looking back at the Cooper that we now know, the idea that he could share a stage with anyone is preposterous. His size, his presence…

The accusation is that Cooper nicked Frankie's best gags, hogged the spotlight, the usual.

'I think I was bewildered more than anything,' said Frankie. 'He just had to be centre stage all the time. He couldn't bear anyone else to get a laugh. It took me by surprise, because when we first met I thought what a charming man he was. We were in a central pool of artists – comedians, dancers, jugglers – and I was quite aware of him because he was making quite a name for himself. We used to do gags together, not as a double act, just bits and pieces. There was a Wild West thing we did where we pushed the salon doors open and we came in with me sitting on his shoulders doing his voice.' The first Tommy Cooper impersonator?

'We got on very well because he didn't see me as a threat to him, but when the top brass tried to put us together his attitude changed. I don't know where all the venom came from.' For Frankie Lyons, at the time it wasn't such a terrible thing. 'I was a 20-year-old sheet-metal worker and I was having the time of my life.' For Frankie Lyons later… It's only later that you start to think 'Why them? Why not me?' but that's a question that people like Cooper never have to ask because they're driven by an internal engine that just won't stop.

Supporters – apologists – would argue that that drive is the price you have to pay for being given the talent, that it's a celestial trade-off, the result of a bargain made somewhere else. I think there is probably some truth in that.

'It's no way an exposé of Tommy Cooper,' Garry said at the time. 'In fact, the play really isn't about Tommy Cooper at all. It's more about the thwarted ambition and unfulfilled dreams of my father. Cooper exists as a kind of foil, like Mozart in *Amadeus*.' Oooh. Shut that door. There was a built-in irony which none of the reviews of the day failed to pick up on. Cooper is such a larger-than-life character that even in *Frankie And Tommy* it is his character that dominates. What chance that it was ever going to be any other way?

'I went out for a meal last night. Ordered everything in French. It surprised everyone. It was a Chinese restaurant.'

The Cooper Curse, pt 2: Wag the Dog

Tommy was away from home on tour and Gwen received a package in the post from the hotel where he was staying. It was a bra and an unsigned note saying that it had been found in Tommy's room. What was this? A 'well-wisher'? A touch of blackmail? Gwen's emotions ran from dumbstruck to furious as she read the note. Her temper rising, Gwen picked up the bra and... cracked up. It had three cups. Another idiot joke shop prank.

YOU'RE MARRIED TO THE PERSON who, in every way, you consider your soulmate. No, you don't consider them your soulmate, you know it. You've been married nearly 40 years, you've got two lovely children, grandchildren, a lovely home, the career's a big success, you've got money coming out of your ears... You've got the type of life where, to anyone looking in, there are two possibilities. Either you were a badly-treated cockroach in a former life and this is pay-back time or you've indulged in some serious religious bribery. Or maybe you're just a lovely person and you deserve all the luck you can get.

You're the sort of couple who say things like 'We finish each other's sentences, don't we, dear?' You're the sort of person who says things like, 'If people ever talk to me about love at first sight, I point to myself.'

Gwen and Tommy Cooper were like that. Two peas. She was one of the few people who didn't laugh that night. She was one of the few people who

Tommy with daughter Vicky and wife Gwen in 1981.

knew immediately. 'We went through his routine in our home like we always used to do,' said Gwen. 'I timed him with the little kitchen clock I use when I bake sponge cakes and things. He had seven minutes to fill and we timed the act to the last second. I remember we argued about how much time would be taken up by the audience laughing. Before he left to go to the theatre, he came to our bedroom and kissed me five times. Then he left with his flask of coffee and lamb and egg mayonnaise sandwiches. I didn't go because I wanted to see how it looked on the box. And it seemed to be going perfectly until he put on that cloak, that beautifully-made cloak for the last trick. It was going to end – and I'm not giving away any secrets – with him producing a great long ladder from under the cloak. And then, when he didn't do that, I knew. I knew.'

It's a funny thing, isn't it. Some things you know instinctively, and some things... some things you just haven't got a clue about. Maybe you know instinctively about things that you know will happen. And what happened next, Gwen, she didn't know it was going to happen, but it was another arrow aimed at that chink in the armour.

Gwen Cooper first heard of Mary Kay when, shortly after Tommy's death, a newspaper contacted her – newspapers, bless them – for her opinion. Her opinion on what? Her opinion on that new book they just were just about to serialise. The book was *For The Love Of Tommy*, by one Mary Kay. Gwen was 'shocked to the very core'.

In her book, Mary Kay claimed to have had an affair with Tommy Cooper for 17 years. A former stage manager at Thames TV, Kay had met Cooper on the set and… It was what neither of them wanted… It was love. They were powerless to resist… He bought me a ring… I loved him devotedly… It was a classic tabloid kiss and tell story. Cooper kissed and Kay told, and did she tell. With her first tabloid cheque, she went out and bought a megaphone.

Meanwhile, in Chiswick…

How could… Was it… Did he… What could Gwen do but deny it? Of course, the mad woman was lying. Of course she was. But then the Cooper children Thomas and Vicky admitted that they knew more than had been said and Gwen's house of cards started to wobble. Cooper's children, Thomas and Vicky. The children often went on tour with their dad. They knew everything that went on, largely because he told them.

Gwen wasn't the only one shocked to the core. This was Tommy Cooper: the great family entertainer. Tommy Cooper, the man who wouldn't tell blue jokes because 'you don't want to go down that road.'

Cooper had millions of fans, all of whom thought that they 'knew' him in that way that viewers think they know their favourite actors and stars. He had been in their living rooms, he'd grown up with them. They'd grown up with him.

Tommy Cooper had been having an affair? For 17 years? What are you talking about? This is the man *The Times* obituary writer described as: 'the crag-featured comedian whose profile seemed carved from a combination of a relief map of Norway, the north face of the Eiger and an Easter Island sculpture.'

This man, he was a sex-dog? Are you serious?

EVEN to people who didn't know Cooper, who didn't care, it was a story that produced a huge shock wave. We're all used to showbiz folk having the morals of a hungry polecat, but this was a family. This was a secure unit. A loving, decades-old marriage, a soulmate deal - and it's a sham? Really, how many people out there in viewerland are secure in loving, decades-old marriages? Makes you think, doesn't it?

The newspapers didn't contact Tommy Cooper's public. They found out in an even more wonderfully bizarre way. Mary told them on Robert Kilroy-Silk's talk show. No, really. He did a show on 'the other woman' and asked for other women to come forward. Mary Kay put her hand up. What followed was a classic tabloid event. Exclusive followed exclusive, claim followed counterclaim. It was messy, ugly and a sad epitaph to a great man. Mary dragged her story through the papers and the papers – in the interests of the public, mind – couldn't help but play along. 'Thomas [Tommy's son] was 15 and I had only just met him when he said, "Promise me, Mary, you won't take Dad away from Mum." I replied, "Don't worry, I promise you I won't – ever." I believe he understood that his father needed us both. He said to me, two years before Tommy died, "Mary, if you ever leave Dad it will be the death of him." Tommy always said, "I can't leave my wife. I won't." His concern was probably over money.'

It got better.

'I wasn't the first other woman in Tommy's life. Before we fell in love I used to answer the phone to a Mrs Smith.'

And better.

'Two weeks before he died he said to me, "When I die, Mary, you won't have to worry about money ever again." He meant to see his solicitor, but died three days before he could keep his appointment.'

And better. Mary talked to the press about their great 'physical' relationship, about how they'd made love the day that Tommy died.

Gwen made reference to the fact that, by that time, Tommy was so ill that he was physically incapable. That he was impotent. 'Tommy was so ill he could barely walk. How could she say that? How could she say she had sex with him? How could she?'

Mary said, 'Oh dear, poor Dove. I do feel sorry for Dove.'

Can you credit all this? These two women, both of whom claim to love Tommy Cooper, dragging his memory through the gutter press, parading his sexual prowess for all to see. It's sad beyond sad.

Later, Gwen rationalised it all with a version of events that suited her. 'Tommy slept with her, but only once. It was in some dressing room somewhere. It was a silly, one-night thing. He knew he'd done something very stupid. But she fell completely in love with him.'

According to Gwen, Mary had been bitten and pursued Tommy, and he was 'too soft-hearted to get rid of her'. Also, she said, he didn't want to get involved in any scandals. It might affect the children. She added, rather needlessly, 'If I'd known about it when he was still alive… I don't know what I'd have done. Not just to him, but to that woman as well.'

'I was cleaning out the attic the other day with the wife. Filthy, dirty and covered with cobwebs… but she's good with the kids.'

Quite what Mary Kay's story really was who knows? It's interesting, though, that in 1991, when Thames TV put together another of its *Tommy Cooper's Greatest Hits* packages, Mary went running to the press saying that she had been a consultant on the show and that she had her name removed from the credits to protect Tommy's widow, Gwen. A Thames TV spokesman said: 'Miss Kay's had absolutely no involvement in the Tommy Cooper shows. Nor does she work for, or with, Thames TV.'

Who knows? What are we talking about here? A woman who was really lived in Big Tommy's heart or someone who's a few tassels short of a fez? I'm not sure and I'm not sure that I want it to be anything more than that. If Mary Kay had had an affair with Tommy Cooper for 17 or however many years, why on earth did she feel the need to

'A man went to the doctor and said, "I need help urgently. I keep dreaming that nude women come into my bedroom and I keep pushing them away." The doctor said, "What do you want me to do?" And the man said, "Cut my arms off."'

Gwen attending Tommy's memorial service.

cash in on it in such a crass manner? Writing a book? Oh, come now, Mary.

Why did you say, 'I wanted people to remember him and I got a bit worried that people were forgetting about him rather quickly. I want people to know more about Tommy and the way he was. I don't want people to be totally in the dark about somebody they loved – and the public did love Tommy. But they knew nothing about him, not the real man'? It's a curious thing. That quote is 64 words long. You could have said the same thing in a much more concise manner: 'I wanted to get my name in the papers'. There. That's only nine words.

Son, Brother and Grandson of the Cooper Curse

Tommy and Thomas in 1983.

TOMMY COOPER MIGHT have been forgiven for thinking that, after the Mary Kay business and the distress that it must have caused to his family, the Angel of Light and Dark would have had its pound of flesh and lifted the Cooper Curse. Some chance.

Where shall we start? Let's start at the beginning. On 16 August 1988, Thomas Cooper died. He was 32.

The *Sun* treated the story with its usual delicacy and respect for the dead: 'Cooper's son was killed by boozing', ran its headline. 'Tommy Cooper's son died from drink, it was revealed…' The story went on to 'report' how Thomas was devastated because, six weeks before, his wife Linda had walked out after a row about his drinking, taking their three children with her. 'Big boozer Tommy junior was devastated when his wife walked after a row over his drinking.' See?

As was by now traditional, the press phoned Gwen for her reaction. It's funny. After Tommy and Mary Kay, she must have dreaded the phone ringing.

What's that going to be? What do they want my reaction about now? 'Thomas was broken-hearted. He allowed his health to get low.'

Allowed his health to get low. Yes, you could say that. He'd been on a life-support machine after his liver had failed. An internal haemorrhage brought on by the booze in a body weakened by gout. To ease the pain, he'd been eating aspirin. Booze, gout, aspirin. It wasn't a good combination. The hospital pumped 70 pints of blood into his body, but it wasn't to be. As quickly as it went in, so it came out. Simply, the blood wouldn't clot. It would have been a bit of a two-bob curse if it was just a case of blood not wanting to clot. You think the Cooper Curse would have put up with that? No. We're looking for something with a bit more meat, a bit more... heartache.

Maybe it's time to hear from one of those 'family friends' so beloved by the tabloid press: 'Thomas died broken-hearted. His wife had just left him and had taken the children with her. He was devastated. He hadn't really eaten properly since she left six weeks ago and had been drinking quite heavily for the past month. Linda filed for divorce and Tom was desperately trying to arrange a reconciliation with her – but his health gave out first.'

A scene was depicted of a family that had disintegrated, a family that had fallen apart. It was all dreadfully sad – dreadfully sad, but not uncommon. He loved her more than she loved him, both drank to compensate their individual feelings, to ease the pain. And the drink made it all worse.

'Linda drank more than was good for her and that led to some dreadful rows,' said the friend. 'She didn't care about causing a scene in front of family or strangers. But in spite of everything he still loved her. Her favourite tipple was extra-strong lager. But Tom was horrified when he took her to her office one day and she stopped off at the supermarket to buy a bottle of vodka.'

At the funeral, Gwen and Linda hardly said a word to each other. Both blamed the other for the tragedy. Gwen, for her part, said she had no idea that things had got so bad. The last time she saw the grandchildren, 'I gave the kids some pocket money and kissed them goodbye. I thought they were just going for a holiday. Then Linda rang to say that they weren't coming back. It was a terrible shock. I had no idea things were as bad as they were. Thomas said that he didn't know what the problem was. He was desperately upset. I've never seen him so hurt.'

AGAIN, when it came to the hard bit, it was Gwen who had to carry the load - though in truth it was probably just as well that it was her. She was used to it by this time. 'I'm glad that Tommy wasn't around. He could not have coped. He'd have fallen to pieces.' After three days of Thomas being propped up by life-support machines, Gwen Cooper had to do something that no parent should ever have to do. She had to give the order to the doctors to switch off.

The press had a field day and talked

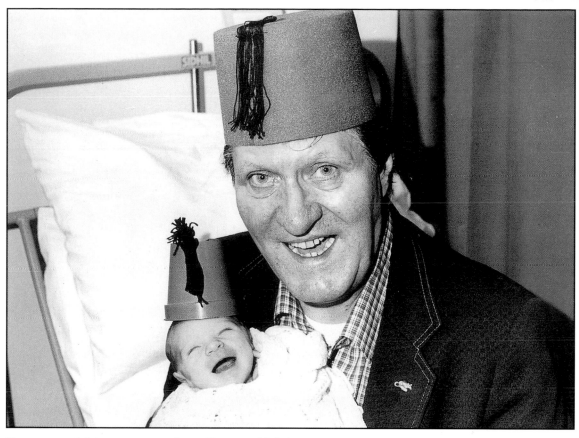

Tommy and his new grandson Tam in 1984.

about 'another victim of the Cooper curse.' Really, they did. You thought it was just me being facetious, didn't you?

Gwen was stoical, strong. It's a common thing. People who are in a very solid relationship, a relationship where both parties depend on each other, outsiders look at them and they think that, if either partner died, the other would collapse. But it doesn't happen. People have enormous reserves of strength and are unexpectedly resilient. Gwen Cooper. Dove. But as she herself said, anyone less Dove-like she couldn't imagine.

This was a woman who'd lived with the loveable maniac who was Tommy Cooper, the woman who'd seen off the Mary Kay storm. But what she had to deal with now was different. For a wife to bury her husband is sad. For a parent to bury her child, it goes against the natural order. 'Tommy was

ill for so long before he died, I was in some ways expecting it. But Thomas? That was, if these things can be compared, the worse of the shocks. He was only 32.'

'His last words to me were, "It's all right mum. I'm tired now. Go home."' So she did. And then so did he.

And if you thought that was enough... On 17 December 1989, the *News Of The World* ran a story headlined - yes, they did - Another Victim Of The Cooper Curse. 'The brother of Tommy Cooper — who dropped dead on TV — has himself died after appearing in a show in which he impersonated the star. Tragedy struck after David Cooper put on the comic genius's famous fez and performed one of the madcap magic routines.' David, ten years Tommy's junior, had inherited his big brother's love of magic and had always wanted to be on the stage, but what Tommy Cooper did, it wasn't like a family business, was it?

The nearest that David came was owning a magic shop in Slough, Berkshire. When a TV producer approached David and said that he was making a Cooper retrospective (Paul Madden's 1990 Channel 4 documentary entitled – can you bear the suspense? – *Just Like That!*) and would he appear and would he put on Tommy's fez and would he perform one of Tommy's idiot magic gags? Well, without wanting to sound harsh, it was like shining the bat-signal up into the sky for The Cooper Curse. They were asking for it.

Speaking from the family's magic shop, David's widow Zena said, 'We're heartbroken. David didn't live long enough to see himself on TV. Fate can be so cruel.'

As Zena pondered what might have been, the surviving members of the Cooper clan were bolting their doors and putting bars on their windows. As they scrambled around, checking out their life assurance policies, Gwen sat back and stared at the phone. Who would they call about next?

She didn't have to wait that long.

'I wonder sometimes why I have to live in one room and why I haven't got a mansion to live in like my grandfather had,' ten-year-old Tam Cooper said in a Sunday paper in 1993. Ten-year-old Tam Cooper? He's ten and he's selling a story to the Sundays? Kids these days, they grow up so quickly. But even so, ten? What was it? Something in the genes?

The story – which took an astonishing six paragraphs before mentioning the words 'Cooper curse' – told the sad tale of Thomas's widow, Linda. Following their divorce and Thomas's subsequent death, Linda had sought a new career in a new bottle – that's a career where opportunities never dry up – and had taken a one-way ride on the misery line to nowhere. Another marriage, another failure. Another home, another failure. Bickering with her mother, bickering with Gwen. Accusation and retribution were the constants. A picture emerged of someone who was less concerned with tenants than Tennent's. A friend – unnamed, obviously – said. 'Tommy would turn in his grave if he could see what was happening now. His dying wish was that his only grandson wouldn't fall foul of the Cooper curse and would have the best in life.' Bournemouth's a nice town, but still. A one-room apartment in a run-down house hardly constitutes the best in life.

NECESSARILY, the press phoned Gwen for her reaction. Wearily, she picked up the phone. As she did so, she mentally ran through the remaining members of her family. 'It breaks my heart not to see my grandson, but if that's what Linda wants I have to respect her wishes. Tam is my only grandson, but his mother is adamant that she wants to bring him up her way.'

'I'm sure Gwen could find us if she wanted to.' (Linda)

'She only has to pick up the phone and I'll help in any way I can.' (Gwen)

And on and on and on.

Tommy Cooper left young Tam

£40,000 but there was a stipulation that he couldn't get his hands on it until he was thirty. Maybe Tommy knew more than he let on. Maybe he could see into the future. Maybe someone - or something - gave him an insight into what might happen after his death. The Ghost Of Curses To Come?

Gordon Williams was a regular sort of amateur magician. Happy rather than successful, Gordon was a baker who indulged himself in a touch of the old 'pick a card, any card' caper. His hero, naturally, was Tommy Cooper. Who else was it ever going to be? One day, he remarked to his wife, 'When I die, I hope it's just like Tommy Cooper went – on stage, surrounded by laughter.'

Gordon. No.

On 25 April 1997, the *Daily Star* ran a small news piece headlined, Tommy Fan Goes Just Like That. Williams, it transpires, got his wish when he had a massive coronary while performing. In a bizarre repeat performance, the crowd laughed as Gordon's partner Paul McCaig tried to revive him, unaware of the tragedy that was unfolding before their eyes. As Paul frantically called for the house lights to come up, the truth slowly dawned on the audience. 🎩

Gwen after Tommy's death.

'A woman phoned her husband and said, "The carburettor is full of water." "Where's the car?" the man said. "In the river," she replied.'

A Man Out of Time

THE LAST SERIES OF *Cooper's Half Hour* was in 1980. There were no shows in 1981, 1982 or 1983. In a way, this isn't surprising. He maintained a presence by doing the odd guest appearance, a slot here and there, a variety show when there was such a beast – which wasn't often, for if there was a beast less in sync with his time than Cooper, it was the variety show. Even without knowing anything more about Cooper, you just know that the early 1980s weren't his time.

Young radicals on the make, moaning about Thatcher and looking for a career, that was the early 1980s. Tommy Cooper coming on stage with a pair of glasses with antlers on the side and saying, 'Horn-rimmed glasses', well, that wasn't going to bring down the Tory bastards, was it? The revolution that was punk had not only blown away past musical forms deemed by the new order to be 'dinosaurs', it had devoured everything else that the light touched. If Mao hadn't nicked the phrase first and given it it's Death Row image, we could say that it was a bit of a cultural revolution. But that's what it was.

Like some ravenous, out-of-control Frankenstein's monster, punk went searching in and around the crevices of social and cultural life, searching out dinosaurs to destroy. Appear in the wrong jeans or the wrong shirt and you'd destroy whatever it was you were trying to say. Hair parted in the wrong way and that was it. (What do you mean, your hair was parted? It was long enough to part? Hippie!) Music obviously was the cultural yardstick, but everything – film, theatre, telly… everything was hit. Everything was affected. It was a real baby-and-the-bathwater deal. If anyone had thought about it, Cooper would have probably been thrown out on account of his hair being too long. Well, I mean, be fair. It came down over his ears. Bleedin' hippie.

More than any of his contemporaries, Cooper was untouched by the vagaries of time and fashion. Unlike people like Bruce Forsyth – I don't know if you've ever seen any footage of Bruce Forsyth doing *The Generation Game*… It's to die for, though to be fair the only thing from that era that Bruce has kept is the sideburns. They've been recycled and now sit on top of his head. Anyway there isn't any old footage of Cooper with him wearing embarrassing clothes. Well, OK, he once appeared on Bob Monkhouse's chat show wearing a full set of chicken legs. Didn't seem embarrassed, though.

Consciously or not, Cooper knew that if you make no attempts to be fashionable, you can never be out of fashion. Tommy Cooper dealt with punk's cultural revolution in exactly the same way that

he'd dealt with it the last time the revolution came to town. He ignored it. In the 1960s, when everyone was running around, giving it loads of peace and love and talking about flower power, Cooper didn't so much go to San Francisco as get a limo to the Wolverhampton Moss Empire. Well, Haight Ashbury didn't have a Moss Empire, did it?

It's a curious thing, but in both those revolutions – and, strangely, in the only other recent popular revolt of any real significance, the dance-culture revolution of the early 1990s – traditional entertainers in dinner suits who addressed the 'Ladies and gentlemen' in the audience were both ignored and excluded.

Of course, they were excluded. Boring old farts. It wasn't even a question.

As far as the cultural czars were concerned, Cooper was irrelevant. Maybe if it had been the early 1990s instead of the early 1980s, Cooper would have been embraced as 'post-modern', 'post-ironic' or some such nonsense the way that, say, Frankie Howerd was. Howerd had been a cultural pariah for the best part of two decades – sexist schmexist, you know – and then, as if by magic, he was dragged out of exile and declared 'alternative'. Bang. There he was down the Hackney Empire and other such temples of cool doing the whole 'Oo-er, missus! Titter ye not!' routine and the only difference between that stuf now and 1973's stuff was that Adrienne Posta wasn't hanging around with (next to) no clothes on.

It was, of course, complete nonsense. Even if anyone knew what those post-this and post-that terms means (and no one does, largely because they don't actually mean anything) they would have just looked stupid next to Tommy Cooper. And he would have made them look even more stupid than they were.

Cooper was untouched because he made no concessions. He made no concessions in the way he looked – a man in a straight dinner suit. That's timeless, isn't it? He made no concessions in the tricky problem about the hair - he wore a hat – and he made no concessions in his material. He didn't bend over and get involved in any idiot game shows. *Play Your Cards Right* and *The Winner Takes All*. To a very real degree, he remained completely untouched by life outside Planet Cooper. His humour ignored both micro politics – the figures of the day, the names, the characters – and macro politics – the trends of the day, feelings towards things like racism and sexism. He didn't only ignore life, he didn't even acknowledge it.

Political correctness? Tommy Cooper was a big fan of political correctness.

Alone among his contemporaries, you could see footage of Cooper and you simply wouldn't be able to date it. When was that show? Who could tell? It was timeless. He looked the same. The set was the same. The gags were the same. It was Tommy Cooper. End of story.

'A man goes into a restaurant and orders a lobster. When it arrives, he complains to the waiter, "It's only got one claw." The waiter says, "It was in a fight." The man replies, "Well, bring me the winner."'

Cigarettes and Alcohol

'If there's one conjuring trick that Tommy does successfully, it's making a drink disappear.'
– Gwen Cooper

THE LAST SERIES of *Cooper's Half Hour* was in 1980, then. No shows in 1981, 1982 or 1983. We've done that bit and we.ve chatted for a while, but we still haven't come to any conclusion about why Cooper all-but disappeared from our screens. As ever, the truth is a relatively simple thing. And as ever, it's not something that you particularly want to talk about. That's what it's like with the truth.

Look. Tommy Cooper was 62 when he died and, fair enough OK, so 62 isn't the first flush of youth but it's not exactly old, either. So you know the only way you'll get to Wimbledon is down the A3, but you're not looking through the Next Life catalogue yet, either.

No, it's not old in the great scheme of things. Let's be honest here. You know that if someone dies when they're 62 they're either dead unlucky or somewhere along the line they've been a naughty boy.

'He rarely appeared in the 1980s,' said Roy Addison, a key figure in the Thames TV press office from 1972 until the end of Tommy's time there, 'and partly it was a fashion thing, but mainly it was because Tommy became too unreliable. The shows became too much like hard work and because they were taking so long to make they became very expensive.'

Once you know The Tommy Cooper Story it somehow seems obvious. It's one of those stories that you think about and you realise you knew it even though you'd never heard it. It's like when you hear a classic pop song, it's like you've heard it before.

The Tommy Cooper Story. How shall we say this? If it were a film it wouldn't be James Stewart, it would be Ray Milland. And, no. He didn't have x-ray eyes.

Tommy Cooper. There he stands in front of a theatrical curtain next to a small table. He picks something up from the table. Puts it down. He tells a rubbish gag. Throws it away. He doesn't sing, he doesn't dance. There are no huge gestures, no acrobatics. He's just there, in front of his curtain.

Maybe you should look a bit more carefully. He's like a Duracell bunny. Watch him on stage and, without knowing anything about him, you just know that this man is a health hazard. He doesn't so much rush around as stress around. He's constantly in motion, making sure everything is going right, making sure that it will eventually go wrong. You can see it with Cooper in a way that you can't with so many others. (Let's not pluck any names out of the air as examples. That would be tempting fate a little too much.) But with Cooper… the constant energy, the constant movement, throwing gags away like they were bits of confetti, getting tricks wrong, screwing up. The constant movement, the sweat, the looking around in mock-panic, the rush… He was like a juggler spinning a dozen plates around.

As Clive James said, 'He threw jokes away the way he threw the juggling away and he threw lines away as if he were consigning them to oblivion, so the line came out as if it wasn't worth saying so you were always leaning forward trying to catch what he was discarding.' It was all a rush, all thrown away. That was another Monsewer Eddie Gray-ism.

TO WORK, Cooper's act needed timing from the gods, it needed to be absolutely perfect, something that Tommy was acutely aware of. It's a sweet irony that if it all worked perfectly, it would manifest itself as a gag going wrong. For a magician to do his business and for it all to go well, that's one thing. But to do all that and then make sure it goes wrong, that's something else. And not only must it go wrong, but it must go wrong in the right way. And at the right time, so that you can throw in all your idiot gags. To do all that and do it perfectly – what margin of error? – that was hard work and Cooper knew it.

'I'll tell you something,' Tommy once said. 'You can buy a box of tricks, you can buy a simple trick from a magic shop and you can know how it's done. Yet a magician can work on that particular trick and make something out of it and you'll think it's not the same trick that you've got. I'll tell you what. Straight magic and funny magic are almost equally difficult. If it's straight, it's very hard and takes a lot of practice, you see. To send it up is still hard, so it's more or less on the same level, although the magic has to go wrong at exactly the right time, so I suppose that actually it is harder.'

And while you're over there, crank that stress-o-meter up a few notches, will you?

It's an accepted part of the magician's game that he tries to distract you so that he can do what he does. The left hand dances and catches the eye so that the right hand can get on with the business of deceit. But Tommy Cooper wasn't like that. More than any other performer I can think of, Tommy Cooper attracted people not because of his act but simply because of him. Over and above the tricks and the fez and the gags, there was an energy and a warmth that attracted people. Looking at Cooper on stage, working, he's constantly in motion. Throwing out gags, tricks. It was, literally, a magnetic energy. Everything about him was energy. He was constantly moving, constantly looking.

Bob Monkhouse recalls Cooper musing about that very thing. 'We were talking about comedians, and Tommy said to me, "That Arthur Askey, he never stops moving around. I love that. All that energy. Never stops moving." And I never asked Tommy, but it was obvious that that's where he got that from. I never saw Tommy where he wasn't moving, where some part of him wasn't moving and the audience fed off that energy.'

It was his energy that consumed those cigarettes, his internal stress-o-meter that demanded that alcohol. Like many larger-than-life performers, Cooper lived off his nerves. Gwen Cooper said, 'He was terrible to live with before the show because he was a bundle of nerves, and after the show he'd buy me bunches of flowers.'

Tommy Cooper pushed himself to the limits. He was driven, and the thing that was driving him was Tommy Cooper.

And after 30-odd years driving, that's a lot of miles.

'Towards the end of his time at Thames, we could barely transmit the shows,' said Roy Addison. 'For every six or seven half-hour shows we broadcast we had to make about ten. Like I say, he just became unreliable. He'd always been extraordinarily bad with time and rehearsals were never like they were with other people, but…'

But what? 'In the later years he wasn't as coherent as he had been, not as focused. He tended to ramble on which, of course, everyone just assumed was part of the act.'

Tommy Cooper was, I guess, a lush. Fine by me. A man works hard, he's entitled to a gin and tonic after a heavy day at the office. Go on then. Have another. What was that? On days when there's a 'y' in the day you have a extra drink? Yeah, 'course.

'I'm on a whisky diet. I've lost three days already.'

But then you ask a bit more and suddenly a picture appears in front of you that's altogether sadder. It's a different picture entirely. 'He'd always been a heavy drinker, always had been,' Addison told. 'To be honest I don't really know what happened, what made him tip over the edge. I suspect that it was just a gradual progression, the sort of thing that happens to a lot of people who drink.

'But,' he continued, 'Tommy was subject to none of the back-biting that normally goes on. Clearly it was effective, because no gossip came out about how Tommy was in the later years because people

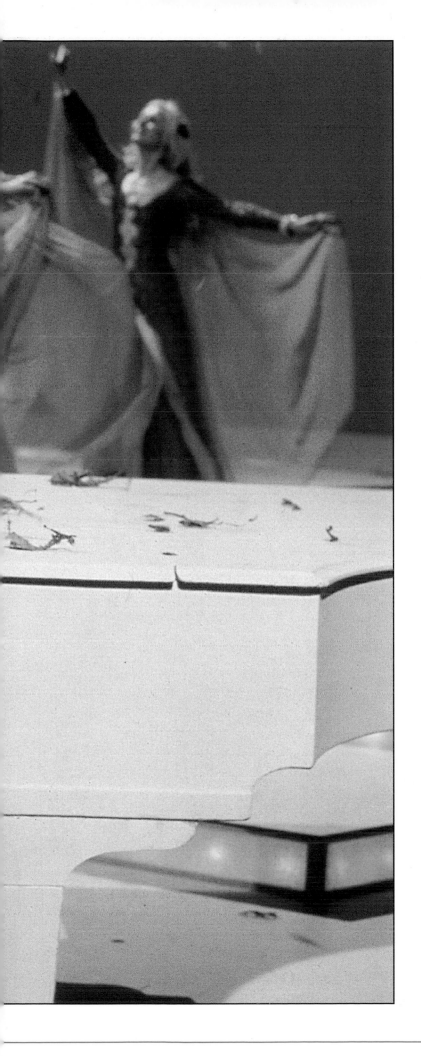

didn't want to talk about it.'

It's a testament to the genuine, almost Masonic, protectiveness of that coterie of comics and entertainers that no stories about Tommy's drinking came out after his death. While he was alive? OK, no one is going to step out of line then, but you'd have thought that after he died, after a reasonable period of respectful silence, a few stories might surface. After all, as far as the tabloid press were concerned, it was open season on Tommy Cooper. The mistress story had already shot a few holes in the image. What price a story on how Tommy Cooper was a lush? But there was nothing. Not even a sneaky 'The Tommy I Knew' by the assistant at the Chiswick branch of Thresher's?

It renews your faith, no?

Dennis Kirkland worked with Tommy Cooper for over 20 years, going from floor assistant to producer/director and taking in most jobs along the way, including a stint as a stand-up warm-up. When I got to meet him and talk to him about Cooper, it was like talking about an old mate, albeit one I'd never met. I didn't want to ask him, but I felt that I had to. There's a thin but important line between acknowledging the truth and hiding it. So I asked him.

'I've got to ask.'

'Ask whatever you like. We're talking about a friend here.'

'What was the drink story?'

'Tommy liked a drink. What do you mean? What was the drink story?'

'Yeah, but how much?'

'I'm not going to tell you that. I can't tell you that. Never knock an artist.'

And after that I didn't ask again. I agreed with Dennis. And anyway, there didn't seem much point.

Have you ever smoked? If you have, you'll know what it's like. It's not something you think about doing, it's just something you do. It becomes part of you, part of your identity. And to try to stop – it's a bitch. If you've never smoked, if you've never given up smoking, try this. Don't blink. Give it, what? What shall I give it, you non-smoking blinker. Try five minutes. Starting from now.

It hurts, doesn't it? You have to think about it, think about it hard. You have to make a conscious decision not to do it and then as soon as you've made that decision, you've got to make another one. And each time you make that decision, it hurts a bit more. But listen. One blink. It's not going to kill you. I'm not looking. One blink and then you'll stop. One blink. You can control that. It's not like you've got to blink. It's not like you need to blink. You're making a controlled, mature decision to blink. You're in control of this thing.

Sorry. I just had to do that. Non-smokers are sometimes the most… well, let's just say it's important to understand the passion involved. Now then, where were we?

You like a drink? It seems a shame to have a drink and not have a smoke. I mean, you're in the pub now. Here have another one. What was that? When there's a 'y' in the day you have a extra smoke? Yeah, 'course.

Think about it. That voice. That laugh. That laugh didn't come from a mouth that reached for the camomile tea when it felt a bit stressed. That voice had lived, it had seen things. Tommy Cooper chain-smoked. Cigars. Popped them down like they were Polo mints or something. It wasn't so much a habit as a career.

Four days before he died, the *Sun,* that bastion of good reporting, ran a story saying that Tommy had been given orders by his doctors to 'Stop smoking or die!'

That there were shades of Eric Morecambe in all this was a little too close for comfort. Morecambe had had the heart attack, he'd had the warnings, he'd had the *Sun* headlines. After one of his doctor's warnings, Eric put a notice in his living room: 'NO SMOKING OR DRINKING BEFORE 7PM'. 'It also says that my limit is one large scotch and two ounces of tobacco a day. I've had a narrow escape with my second heart attack and it's frightening me. I'm going to be very, very careful. When I wake up every morning, I say to myself, "Take care Eric, you've just had another heart attack."'

I leave you to search for the logic in all that. As Eric entered the final furlong, he said, 'I'm not going to give up my pipe, because I really enjoy that. But I am cutting down hard on the booze. I know I was drinking too much.'

All that, it could have been Tommy Cooper. As with Eric Morecambe, the doctor's warning did pull him up a bit. In that interview, Tommy talked about slowing down, about taking time out. Doing the gardening. 'I still enjoy working as much as ever because magic is still my passion just as it has always been. But I want to slow down a bit – you can't go too fast when you get to my age.'

Cooper's smoking was just like you'd think Cooper's smoking was. Hard, fast, manic. And it took its toll.

Tommy revealed that he had given up smoking his precious cigars and had been 'clean' for three months. But then he went on to say that he 'hadn't the faintest idea why people found him funny.' What are you going to do? Buy a quote from a man who used to put trick soap in his bathroom so that his wife would end up with a black face?

Bob Monkhouse: 'Tommy said he'd given up alcohol and smoking, whereupon he cracked open a tin of lager and lit up a cigarillo. I said to him, "Tommy, I thought you said you'd stopped," and he said, "You can't call this drinking," and, taking another drag on the cigarillo, "You can't call this smoking." Nothing could have stopped him. He was an unstoppable man.'

There's nothing you can say that's got any worth. You cannot say, "Oh, if only he hadn't smoked." You cannot say, "Oh, if only he hadn't drunk."

We all know that smoking is bad for you. Well, we do now. It could be argued that, in the days when Tommy Cooper did most of his smoking, we didn't know. Actually, it could be argued that in the days when Tommy Cooper did most of his smoking, we didn't know but maybe 'they', the tobacco companies, did know and just didn't tell us, but that's a different argument in a different book.

This is not to condone smoking or drinking – heaven forbid. They both kill millions needlessly and worthlessly, but it's the essence of the man that's of far greater import than any particular vice. And it's the essence of the man that drove him to those particular vices. If Tommy Cooper hadn't drunk or smoked he might still be alive today, true. But then again, he most probably wouldn't be Tommy Cooper and, quite possibly, never would have been.

A year before he died, Tommy Cooper had to go into hospital to have seven pints of fluid drained from his lungs, the result of years and years of chain-smoking cigars. Seven pints of fluid. How do you fit seven excess pints of fluid into two lungs? It's tempting to get all sanctimonious and rabbit on about government health warnings and the like, but you and I both know that if Tommy Cooper had been faced with the question 'How do you fit seven excess pints of fluid into two lungs?' he'd have come back with a gruff vocal shuffle and a 'Just like that!'. And if that's too glib for you, well, I guess that's your problem. ◼

Tommy Cooper stands in front of his curtain. He is holding a medium-sized brown envelope. 'Inside this envelope is a picture of the world's greatest escapologist, Harry Houdini.' Cooper opens the envelope and pulls out... a blank sheet of paper. 'He got away again.'

Comedy Magic – The New Rock 'n' Roll

'I went to the doctor the other day. I had to. He was ill.'

TOMMY COOPER WASN'T a well man. The drinking aside, the smoking aside, he wasn't a well man. The legs, as already mentioned, were a showbusiness legend. Knotted and gnarled and riddled with varicose veins, stricken with phlebitis and a thrombosis, they were like two runtish pipe-cleaners propping up this huge bear-like body. He also had bad leg ulcers. He always blamed the army, saying that it was all that foot-stamping in the Horse Guards that had caused it.

Like a lot of people who aren't well, Cooper had an extra-sensory perception when it came to his health. Do something practical about it like give up smoking? No. Think long and hard about what disease it might be that you've got? Yes, plenty of time for that one.

His hypochondria was legendary among the family. Said Gwen: 'Whenever he saw someone taking a pill, he would ask for one. He wasn't particularly bothered what it was for, so long as he thought it would do him some good. Once, he nearly took one of the dog's worming tablets when he saw me taking them out. Hotel porters used to make a fortune out of him in tips. He was always sending them for tablets or tissues or some other thing he didn't really need.'

And Vicky: 'Even when I was taking a vitamin pill, Dad insisted on having one. Thomas and I were always planning to get our own back on him. The plan was to produce laxatives from a bottle and make as though to swallow them. We knew Dad would jump up and demand one – and pay the consequences later.'

It's funny. You think of sex and drugs and you think rock 'n' roll. Transit vans up and down the motorway. Rolled up tenners. You don't really think of a mainstream, establishment family entertainer. You don't really think of someone like Tommy Cooper. Looking back, if you wanted to be all smart about it, you'd say that Tommy Cooper never stood a chance. A big man with big appetites. It wasn't as if he were an

accountant or a lawyer. A shoe shop assistant, maybe. 'Size seven, in the brown? I'll just check.'

'The trouble was caused, I think, by his lifestyle,' said Kirkland. 'Going to the clubs and staying out all night and not eating properly. You get a lot of this with comics on tour, you know. They don't eat properly and they don't look after themselves. They do their act and then they're up and awake so they go for a bevvy or two or they go for an Italian meal in the middle of the night and then they'll sleep till five in the afternoon the next day. Then they'll get up and do it again and they don't take care of themselves. Tommy didn't take care of himself. He'd eat, but it wouldn't be good food and it would take him about four hours to eat a plate of fish a chips because he would pick little bits of it rather than eat it in one go.'

It sounds like a student's dream. Up all night, boozing and eating crap food, sleeping all day. Throw in maybe someone you're touring with who maybe you're friendly with... The difference was that a student living that life would be in his/her late teens and, as the young people say, mad for it. There was another difference. After sleeping till five in the afternoon, the student would probably prepare to pay back their loan by playing a bit of pool, having a few drinks and then going to bed. Tommy Cooper would put on a top-class, nerve-jangling show.

The first signs that something was wrong came in Rome in 1977. All things considered, that's not so bad. Thirty years in the business. Thirty years in the mad, pressure-strewn business of show. 'Tommy was in Rome and he had a heart attack,' said Kirkland. 'Well, we think he did. He blamed it on blood pressure – he denied the heart attack strenuously and he had a piece of paper [saying so] which I think cost him £1,000. Some nonsense from an Italian quack.

'He came back from Rome and phoned me up so we arranged to meet in a bar in the King's Road. So he turned up – late, of course – he turned up about five to three and the bar shut at three, but of course the bar stays open to Tom.' A valued customer. 'So he sat down and I said to him, "Are you allowed to drink? Would you like a drink?" and he said, "Yes, I'm allowed a glass of red." So I said OK and he said he'd have a Dubonnet. We sat down and about three bottles later I said, "I thought you said you were only allowed one glass?" and he said, "I've only used one glass."'

And that, by all accounts, is a true story.

Tommy never gave up touring. It was his life and by the end it was just too strenuous for him. Looking back, the drink, the smoke, the heart attack… It's part of a pact that all performers make with the Devil. They get to entertain us and they get all that goes along with that, the fame, the kudos, the ego, the gratification, the wealth. And in return

they get the stress, the strain and the burn-out health grief. For the audience it's maybe a fair trade-off. For the performer…? Who knows? You'll have to ask him. ▮

Tommy Cooper stands in front of his curtain. He is holding a medium-sized brown paper bag. He shows the audience that it is empty.

'Ladies and gentlemen. A live pigeon.'

He blows up the bag, twists it closed and then bursts it with his hands.

A mass of feathers falls out of the bag.

How would you like to die?

'What do you call a gorilla with a banana in each ear? Anything you like. He can't hear you.'

ON 15 APRIL 1984, Tommy Cooper collapsed on the stage of Her Majesty's Theatre and died. But it's a curious thing. At that moment, at the moment, Cooper was both relieved of life and invested with immortality.

Tommy Cooper. He was the one who died on stage.

In all of those celebrity questionnaires that appear in the glossy newspaper supplements, there's always the question that asks, 'How would you like to die?' Invariably, the celeb comes back with something warm and gentle like 'in my sleep' or something smart like 'quickly'. One day, I'm going to be asked to fill in one of those questionnaires and, at the moment, my favourite answer is 'Not yet'. My mazel, someone will say that the week before. Still. Tommy Cooper. It's a comfort to know that if Tommy Cooper had filled in one of those questionnaires, the chances are that he'd have replied, 'On stage, making people laugh.'

Tommy Cooper wasn't the first comic to die on stage – and, no, we're not talking about comics who don't get any laughs. The great Sid James, one of the best comedy actors England has ever seen, died while performing a play called *The Mating Game* in Sunderland in 1976. Like Tommy, he collapsed on stage and died on the way to the hospital.

Kenneth Horne, known to an earlier generation as the star of the radio show *Round The Horne*, died while hosting a TV awards show in 1969. Like Cooper, he was going through his routine when he swayed forward and keeled over. The 750 guests at the Dorchester Hotel thought it as part of the act and carried on laughing and applauding. Though it was being filmed, the show wasn't going out live and the BBC had the opportunity to edit out Horne's final exit, stage left.

For a comedian, a performer, what could be better? Your final act. It's a touch Dr Phibes, the grand melodramatic gesture. But performers –

you know what they're like: ego merchants.

As Thomas, his son, said shortly afterwards, 'He was always known for his timing and that was the best bit of timing he has ever done. If I had said to him, "You are going to drop dead tonight in front of millions of people," he would have replied, "I'll settle for that." That was the way he was. It would have tickled him that even his final act raised a laugh.'

Sure, it's sad when someone dies, especially if they die at a comparatively early age. Sixty-two. What's that? You're barely in the final furlong. There's so much left to do, so much left to say. Things that you could have done.

For Tommy Cooper, I'm not sure that there was anything else. He'd been living at such a fast pace for so long, if he'd have stopped his body would have probably revolted. It would have just been too confused. No, I don't think it was likely Tommy was ever going to do anything else.

Eric Morecambe, another burn-out who had it snatched away too soon, was different. He'd written a couple of children's book, he had dreams of becoming a radio personality, like Frank Muir or something. Grow old gracefully. How was Tommy Cooper going to grow old gracefully? The only way that he could have done that would have been to stepped back completely from the public eye, and for someone who'd been performing all their life what would that have been like? He'd been more or less off the screens since 1980 and what good had that done him? For someone like Cooper, someone to whom performing is a way of life, to be robbed of it is to be robbed of oxygen. Ask Ernie Wise. It leaves a hole that eats away at the soul, a hole that consumes.

As the cliché has it, clichés are only clichés because they're true, and as if to prove it, here's a true cliché. It's only sad for those left behind. For those who are doing the dying? For Gwen Cooper, Tommy's dying was sadder than sad. Two peas, remember. Maybe if she'd have been with him. Maybe. For Tommy, though, it was the perfect exit and it guaranteed him a place in showbiz folklore. Tommy Cooper. He died on stage. He died as he lived, with people laughing at him.

Before anyone gets too maudlin about Cooper's death, it's worth remembering one thing. As the spirit of life left his body, it did so to the sound of laughter and applause and calls for more.

It was, apparently, one of Tommy Cooper's quiet boasts that he had never 'died' on stage. Well, as Eric Morecambe might have said, there's not a lot you can say to that. ◼

A man goes to the doctor. The doctor tells him that he has three minutes to live.
'Doctor, what can you give me?' the man says.
'A hard-boiled egg,' says the doctor.

Seven Minutes to Midnight

'I went out and I said to my wife, "I'll be back about 8.40pm," because I thought that Tommy would be topping the bill and I wanted to see his act. So I got back and she said, "You missed it." And I said, "No!" and she said, "Yes, he only did the first part of the show," and I switched on and saw that Tarby was doing a spot and you could see that he was doing one off the top of his head and I thought, "He's had to throw a spot here. What's going on?" So I asked my wife and she said that Tommy just sort of fell over right at the end and I said, "Tommy doesn't fall over." Then my assistant called and she said, "Dennis, something's wrong. Tommy just fell over at the end of the act and they covered him with the curtains." About half an hour later, I got a call from his son, Thomas. He said, "I don't know how to tell you, but dad's dead. Could you tell Eric and whoever..." I just couldn't believe it. I just couldn't believe it.'
– Dennis Kirkland

TOMMY COOPER HAD for a while been conspicuous by his absence. 'Life with Cooper' was, by 1984, strictly a domestic affair. Shows came and went, but rarely did they come with Tom on board. In early 1984, though, his old mucker Jimmy Tarbuck persuaded him to come on and do a guest slot on a Sunday night show he was compering. Tommy Cooper both jumped and held back. Maybe it was first-night nerves, something that he hadn't really experienced since those long gone days when he was in the army.

Maybe he had something to be nervous about. It's said that when the Grim Reaper comes looking, you can hear his footsteps. Maybe Tommy knew things were set to get spooky.

'One day he phoned me up,' tells Dennis Kirkland, 'and it was Friday and he was doing *Live From Her Majesty's* on the Sunday - and he phoned me and said, "Dennis, where have you been? I've been trying to get you all day." And I said, "I've been here, Tom," and he said, "You haven't. I've been phoning and I haven't been able to get hold of you." So I said, "How did you get through to me?" So he said, "I asked the only person who would know," and I said, "Who's that, then?" and he said, "The Duke of Edinburgh." Typical Tommy. You ask him a question and that's what he comes back with.

A young Tarbuck.

Anyway, so I said, "OK, what do you want?" and he said, "I've got to speak to Eric. I've got to speak to Eric." Eric Sykes, you know. So I said, "I'll get Eric, don't worry. What's the problem?" And he said, "I'm doing *Live From Her Majesty's* on Sunday and I haven't got a finish to the act." Well, he had the biggest finish of all time, didn't he? But isn't that sad?'

It was just another show, just another Sunday night show that filled in a few hours between *Songs Of Praise* and the news. And it was about just as memorable. What can anyone remember about that show? One of the co-stars was Donny Osmond. It was that memorable.

What was astonishing, though, was the reaction – and subsequent performance – of Jimmy Tarbuck. The compere for the show, Tarbuck had been umbilically linked to Cooper for years and it was a relationship based on simple respect.

Tarbuck and Cooper had first crossed paths in 1964 when they shared a dressing room together at the *Royal Command Performance*. Tarbuck was a young gun of 23, smart and lippy like 23-year-olds are supposed to be. A Scouse gag machine. Cooper, by contrast, was an old hand and recognised Tarbuck for what he was. He took him under his not inconsiderable

wing and cemented a friendship.

Part of the same old school, the comedy establishment which drew in people like Monkhouse and Forsyth and Sykes, which went back and embraced people like Dickie Henderson and Kenny Lynch, which revolved around charity golf tournaments and arcane organisations like the Grand Order of the Water Rats, it was Tarbuck who was the support, Tarbuck who was happy to play stooge to Tommy those fateful last seven minutes.

The advice that Eric Sykes had given Tommy was to do the cloak gag. 'You haven't done that for a while, Tom.' The cloak gag is that old chestnut where Cooper stands in front of a curtain wearing a cloak and starts bringing out objects that are under the cloak. The usual nonsense that would embarrass a three-year-old.

'A child of three can do this trick. I wish he was here now.'

'As usual, he was supposed to make a mess of the last trick,' said Tarbuck. 'He was wearing a long cloak and said, "There's no trapdoor here." Then a ladder came through his legs, followed by a milk churn and a long pole. Finally, I was supposed to clamber between his legs and on to the stage.'

Tarbuck, who was standing in the wings watching the monitor and waiting for his cue, saw Tommy lean forward and rest on his table for a few long moments and then collapse. 'When Tommy fell backwards, I thought he'd put another gag in. I thought he was going to do some levitation trick from under his cloak. We all expected him to get up and we waited for the roar of laughter. It was terrible when he didn't.'

A blond assistant went to help him with his magic cloak. An eyewitness said, 'She tied it around his neck and walked off, but as she turned away all of a sudden he crumpled. His head went back and everyone heard a snoring sound. No one knew if it was a joke or not.'

A spokesman for the theatre said, 'Everyone was laughing – they thought it was part of the show. It wasn't until Tommy didn't get up again that we realised that something was wrong.'

One person knew. When Tommy Cooper collapsed on the stage of Her Majesty's Theatre on 15 April 1984, the millions watching thought it was another of Cooper's madcap skits. It was typical of the great physical clown, to use his body as a prop to get a laugh. One person watching knew immediately that it wasn't part of any sketch.

Gwen Cooper had spent the bulk of her adult life helping Tommy with his gags, timing him as he practised in the lounge. She knew as well as he did how the act was meant to go, how long each gag was meant to last, how one gag would fall into the next.

It wasn't that Tommy was as rigid as someone like Frankie Howerd who, and this is something of an open secret now, had every 'Ooh-er, missus' and 'Titter ye not' written into a watertight script. Tommy wasn't as nuts-and-bolts as that. It's just that for the gags to go wrong in exactly the right way, they had to be perfectly timed. So while, for example, it would be written that a particular sketch would last two minutes, the words that went into that two minutes would be flexible.

If anything unscripted happened, Gwen knew. 'I knew, of course, that he had to watch his health, but I didn't know, I didn't realise, just how ill he was.'

An ambulance was called and took him the two miles from the West End theatre to Westminster Hospital. One of the ambulancemen said, 'I knew he was dead as soon as we saw him. There was nothing anyone could do.' Ten minutes later at 8.40pm, Tommy Cooper died. Tommy's son Thomas accompanied him to the hospital and telephoned Gwen, who was still at home in Chiswick.

Meanwhile, neither the live theatre audience nor the watching TV audience were told anything and, in true theatrical style, it was on with the show. There's no business like showbusiness. Really, though, what else could they have done? What would have been achieved by making a song and dance about something that was, essentially, a personal tragedy? There would be plenty of time for all the obits, plenty of time for everybody to get sad.

And, nonsense and showbizzy as it sounds, you can't help but feel it's what Tommy would have wanted.

After the impromptu ad break, it was Tarbuck – numb, dumbstruck Tarbuck - who went back on stage and filled in with a two and a half minute stand up slot. I say, I say, I say. My best mate's just keeled over…

REMEMBER, neither TV nor theatre audience knew anything about what had happened, so they had no reason to suspect that Tarbuck shouldn't be there doing a stand-up. While that meant that no one was watching him and thinking, 'Oh my God. How's he going to react?' I still can't help but think that words like professionalism seem ridiculously inadequate to describe Tarbuck's performance. 'I really don't know how I continued,' he said. 'I really can't answer that. I don't really remember what I did.' Tarbuck didn't know that Cooper was dead, not really.

'They didn't tell me that he had died, but I could tell it was serious.' He could tell it was serious. You've been asked to do a couple of minutes because your mate's just keeled over, you glance back behind the curtain and, amid the scenes of panic, you can see your manager trying to revive him giving him the kiss of life…

Then after his slot, 'when I went backstage one of the first aid people was giving him the kiss of life. It was numbing.' He could probably tell it was serious, alright.

The problem was that Tommy was such a big man that they had difficulty lifting him on to a stretcher. Two young comics were due on next, but they couldn't get their gear on to the stage because a prostrate Cooper was in the way. They did their act anyway. Headlining was the veteran American singer Howard Keel, a solid old pro who did what he had to.

'After the show they told me that Tommy had died. I was numb,' said Tarbuck. 'Yet the strangest feeling was the following Sunday when I walked on to the set. I thought, "It was only this time last week that I was roaring with laughter at him and now I've been to his cremation." I find it so hard to believe he's gone.'

ALTHOUGH he wasn't a great gardener, Tommy Cooper loved flowers, daffodils in particular. Numbed to his actions, Thomas came home from his father's funeral, looked at the urn that contained his ashes, looked at the daffodils smiling at him in the garden, looked at the urn again and then opened the back door and walked into the garden. A few minutes later, he walked back inside and threw the urn away. It had served its purpose.

It's such a lovely way to dispose of a body. Cemeteries are all well and good, but they are dreadfully cold places. Special areas purpose-built for death. To put your loved ones ashes in your garden… I know to some people that will sound irreverent and somehow irreligious, but I can't help but feel that there's a certain poetry there. Every year now when the daffodils bloom again, Gwen can look out of her windows and see, well, she can see whatever she wants to.

That's the strange thing about death. One way or another, our lives are surrounded by it. There's the tragedy and the grief and the sadness and all those tangible emotions that we associate with death – but these are emotions that somehow we've subconsciously prepared ourselves for – or rather, they're emotions that we've been prepared for. Every time we switch on the television, every time we turn on the radio, every time we open a newspaper – death. And we read the stories and we see the pain and we see those touched by the death, grieving, emoting, coping. And we ourselves feel touched by their sadness. The chances are that you probably felt that way when you read that Tommy Cooper had died.

For those not directly involved, it's a safe emotional outlet. We feel sad and touched but there's always another story to read and we move on. It's the way that we deal with the news – death, destruction, turmoil. And finally, a cat stuck up a tree.

But put what you might call real life to one side for a moment. Anyone who's had someone near and dear die – and, one way or another, that's just about everyone – knows how weird the whole thing is. After all the sadness has subsided, you're left with the slightly surreal idea that you'll never see that person again. You'll never hear that voice, smell that smell. You'll never walk down the street and see them coming towards you…

Soon after Tommy's death, Gwen gave an interview in which she talked about the feeling of loss. 'Sundays are the worst. I was so used to going to collect him from an airport or a station. Not to have him with me on those days is real murder. He'd always ring beforehand and tell me what he wanted to eat. And he'd ring me every night at seven before he went on stage. Now, when the phone goes at that time I expect it to be him.'

'It's been so lonely, even though there are always plenty of people around me. Sometimes it gets as though there's nothing to look forward to. But I'm trying. I have to, don't I?'

Ladies and Gentlemen, Goodnight

'For most people, life is a bloody grind. They do jobs that they hate – if they are lucky enough to have jobs. So when someone comes along who makes them forget their troubles, it's a relief for them. 'There is something about me that makes people giggle. I honestly don't know what it is and I don't want to know, because maybe if I became too self-conscious I'd lose the gift. All I ask I that when I pop off, people will say, "Tommy Cooper? He was a right scream, that bloke."'

Tommy Cooper? He was a right scream, that bloke.